THE INNER CITY - CAUSES AND EFFECTS

Andrew Kirby

School of Planning Studies

University of Reading

RETAILING AND PLANNING ASSOCIATES

Published by:

R.P.A. (Books)
P.O. Box 5
Corbridge
Northumberland
England

ISBN   0 905269 04 7

Printed in Great Britain by J. & P. Bealls Ltd.,
Newcastle upon Tyne

T H E   I N N E R   C I T I E S

contain:

7% of British population   -   3,800,000 people.

14% of the unskilled workers;

20% of the households in housing stress;

33% of the Commonwealth immigrants;

Unemployment running at twice the national average;

*Employment opportunities contracting at over twice the
national average;*

*Up to ten times the national proportion of families
living below the Supplementary Benefit poverty line.*

*Up to four times the domestic overcrowding found
elsewhere in cities;*

Over twice the national average of single-parent families;

Less than half the national rate of car-ownership.

ACKNOWLEDGEMENTS

I would like to thank the following individuals and organisations for permission to use the following material: Professor John Goddard for Tables 1 and 2; Her Majesty's Stationery Office for information incorporated in Tables 3 and 5; Dr. Graham Lomas for data used in Tables 4 and 5, and Peter Gripaios for Table 6. Full reference to the sources of these Tables is to be found within the text.

C O N T E N T S

L I S T   O F   T A B L E S

F I G U R E S

INTRODUCTION

The 'inner city crisis' is now genuine colour
supplement fodder, even though the photographs are
always in black and white, in order to achieve that
little extra impact. A recent study of Glasgow had a
spread of familiar scenes: broken windows, weary faces,
posed dossers, all sandwiched between a travelogue on
Crete, and a large advertisement explaining "how to gain
more benefit from nature's lavish gifts."
   This sort of interest, all sensation and no analysis,
has produced a weary cynicism amongst some observers
concerning the whole question of inner area policy
making. The Community Development Project talks of a
"new growth industry, providing lucrative jobs for
academics and professionals dedicated to the diagnosis
and treatment of the 'urban crisis'. It is a game of
numbers in which the prize for greatest deprivation
goes to the areas with the highest scores".
   There is more than a grain of truth in this. A
great deal of analysis has fallen into the trap that
the Government has already experienced: "they have
looked at the maps, collected the census data, chosen
areas, and run them through computers checking for social
malaise indicators: unemployment, poverty, illness, crime,
immigrants, deviancy". This is a trap I have tried to
avoid. There are no maps in this monograph, for example.
Instead, I have tried to follow the dictum that "the city
cannot be analysed except as part of society." I have
attempted to get to grips with the more basic questions
of how the inner city problems come about, whom they
affect, and with less assurance, how they might be
solved. I hope that I have observed Ray Pahl's
strictures concerning the "dangers in a *geographical*
analysis of the distribution of social malaise, or more

7

simply, crime and poverty." I would indeed not wish
to collude in the process of trying to limit the size
of the problem in hand "by focussing only upon those
problems which have the most obvious spatial manifestations".

In scope, the book is pitched at a fairly general
level, although I have offered more detailed footnotes in
several places for the interested reader. Nonetheless,
the work is not intended as anything other than a review:
a more detailed analysis is required, but yet to appear.

Several acknowledgements must be made at this juncture.
I would like to thank Ross Davies for asking me to write
this book, and colleagues at Reading for support during a
brief but intensive gestation period. Particular thanks
go to Sheila Dance and Brian Rogers for the diagrams,
Sue Jeffs for the cover layout and to Elizabeth Denny,
who not only gave up a large number of Saturdays to type
the manuscript, but also went to the lengths of buying
me a new pen so that she might be able to read my hand-
writing. The manuscript was criticised by Lyn Davies,
Mick Griffiths and Peter Hall, and edited by Ross Davies:
as always, any sins of ommission or commission remain
mine alone. And as always, thanks to Sue, who has put
up with it all both for four years in Benwell, and now
the Thames Valley.

Cholsey, Oxon. February, 1978.

*"Take them Gorbals-wards, Tom. Take
them Scotland Road-wards. Take them
to deprived sores of inner cities,
urban pustules. Take them to Soweto.
Or live in the Thames Valley, thank
your lucky stars, and shut up".*

David Nobbs, 'The Return of Reginald Perrin'

Chapter One

A   T O T A L   A P P R O A C H

INTRODUCTION

This chapter is an attempt to answer the simple
question "why?"; why have local authorities, political
parties, planners and researchers suddenly become
concerned with the problems of the inner city - that
decaying area that you see as your train pulls out of
the central station of any British industrial centre?

Any observer might be excused for thinking that
this interest, like the 1978 Inner Urban Areas Bill,
is recent. The Government has however spent nearly
two million pounds in the last four years on inner city
research; as Reg Freeson, the Minister for Housing
observes in the preface to the results of this research,
*"it is well over a decade since some of us started to
advocate a 'total' approach to urban renewal, urging
that this should be brought to the centre of politics,
rather than continue as a peripheral issue"*.[1]

The flurries of publicity that have surrounded the
publication of these Reports, and the ensuing White
Paper, tend then to mask a long-standing problem, and
even long-standing attempts to find a solution. As
Peter Hall observes, *"the politicians tend to rediscover
the urban poor every half-decade or so"*.[2] It may be
useful to examine this statement for a moment, in order
to understand better the present policies.

Area Improvement Policies

It has been well-understood for a long-time now
that *social problems*, in the widest sense, may be manifest
as *spatial problems*. At the simplest level, this means
that particular groups tend to cluster together in

identifiable locations. This happens at all scales:
we think of underdeveloped nations, or concentrations
of regional unemployment. The same applies at the
urban scale. We know of racial segregation, and of
religious enclaves. We are also all familiar with
different types of neighbourhoods - some obviously
select, some equally obviously run-down.

In themselves, such concentrations or clusters of
people are not problems. Religious groups may find
strength in segregation, and in the same way, it used
often to be suggested that the poor may find support
from 'the community' within predominantly low-income
areas. The overwhelming impression gained from accounts
of such areas by writers like Frankenberg[3] and Hoggart[4]
is one of stability, and mutual co-operation.

The fact however that groups may find some benefit
in segregation does not discount the fact that some
areas are less desirable than others. In the urban
context, it has become increasingly obvious that the
oldest parts of the cities, the old core areas, have
become poor environments. The facilities that were built
alongside the original houses are now obsolete: the
schools for example reflect different educational
principles. Streets were not built for children and
parked cars, and this is not to overlook the conditions
of the homes themselves, or general job opportunities.

It is within this context that Government area
improvement policies have operated. They have implicitly
connected the existence of the poorest households with
the areas of the greatest decay, and have attempted to
aid these financially weak social groups through the
provision of a better physical environment. In a study
of the inner city, we can trace two distinct types of
improvement policy. One is associated with housing
issues, and as such involves an inner area component
only in so far as the worst housing has traditionally

been found there. ⚡The second, in contrast, has focussed
specifically upon deprivation and malaise within the
cores, and has typically involved 'action projects'
designed both to effect improvements and increase
research knowledge concerning issues such as education.

Within the housing field, the last decade has seen
a move away from wholesale clearance schemes followed
by population resettlement, in either new inner city
estates or suburban overspill schemes. Although the
intentions of those planners promoting clearance are
today being re-evaluated, there is little doubt that
the net result of many clearance schemes was disruption
and planning blight. Partly in response to these
failings, and partly due to changing economic circumstances,
emphasis has increasingly been placed upon the renovation
of dwellings, rather than demolition. Two main items of
legislation, the Housing Acts of 1969 and 1974, provide
for the existence of General Improvement Areas (GIAs),
and Housing Action Areas (HAAs). The former consist
of small areas of perhaps five hundred houses, where
an essentially stable population is thought to be
capable of benefitting from the provision of grants for
home improvement. In addition, the local authority
provides parking spaces, creates play streets, plants
trees and provides general environmental improvement.
HAAs, on the other hand, are declared in areas of
greater social stress, where for example larger numbers
of families are concentrated within privately rented
accommodation, (which is frequently in very poor condition).
Provision exists for slum clearance, home improvement
and more general attention.

In contrast to the housing strategies, the so-
called 'poverty programme' has a deliberate inner city
content. A lineage can be traced back to the famous
reports of the sixties: Milner-Holland, Seebohm and
Plowden. The first examined London's housing, the

second the social services, whilst Plowden dealt with
the educational problems of children from deprived
backgrounds. From the Committee's report emerged the
experiment of Educational Priority Areas, which like
the GIAs and HAAs already discussed, attempted to provide
positive discrimination to small areas, in this instance
by increased spending within primary schools on salaries
and equipment. From initial trials between 1968 and
1971, the EPA scheme has been extended throughout the
country to many inner city schools.

Numerous experiments have followed the EPA trials.
In 1969 the Home Office set up twelve Community
Development Projects, designed to jointly find out
more about the problems of deprived communities, whilst
encouraging greater self-help and participation from
the residents, and improved small area management from
the local authorities in question. The enthusiastic
teams working in a variety of locations from Liverpool
and Newcastle through to Oldham and Glyncorrwg have
produced a flood of reports, but until its final closure
in 1977 the National CDP adopted a stance essentially
contrary to that of the Government, by emphasising the
problems of area-based discrimination, a point that I
shall return to extensively in the following Chapters.

Since the inception and eclipse of the CDPs, a
series of alternative area-based experiments have been
set up. Some, like the Inner Area Studies already
cited, were financed by the Department of the Environment
and emphasised research, rather than action projects
like play schools or community groups. Others, like the
Comprehensive Community Programmes, were intended to
improve local authority management skills. Over the
years, different bodies have sponsored different types
of schemes. The Community Relations Department within
the Home Office has financed the Urban Aid Programme,
which has spent a steady £4 million pounds per annum

since 1968 on small-scale requirements for voluntary
groups and local authority schemes. The Home Office
also possesses the Urban Deprivation Unit, which
promoted the ill-fated CCPs and a Deprived Areas
Project in conjunction with the Greater London Council.
At the time of Conservative Government, the Department
of Health and Social Security also set up research into
the field of deprivation transmitted from generation to
generation.

This confusing list of abbreviations represents
only a part of the last decade's measures designed to
provide information or solutions to area-based poverty
within the inner city. Whilst several of these
schemes will be discussed below, a full list of projects,
such as the finance offered by the EEC, would represent
an over-long catalogue, not least because of their rapid
obsolescence.[5]

A Changing Background

When we look back over nearly a decade of moves
designed to overcome deprivation, and look forward to
major initiatives designed to deal with urban problems,
we must conclude that the existing policies have failed.
This is true, but must be extensively qualified.

Essentially, we must recognise that all the moves
made so far have been aimed at the fabric of the
problems: the buildings, the houses, the environment.
As such, the investment has existed in a vacuum, outside
considerations of economic or social policy in general.
In the last three or four years however these 'background'
issues have shifted dramatically. The most important is
the major downturn in the western economies: the worst
since 1945. Unemployment has risen to unprecedented
post-war levels, with firms closing at an abnormally high
rate. In each case, the weakest within society suffer,
and in each case, as we shall see, there is a good deal of

evidence that the main sufferers are those in the
urban cores. In many senses, then, the problems of
physical decay have been given an added, social dimension.

. Secondly, we have become more conscious of racial
overtones within society at large. Government legislation,
embodied in the Race Relations Act, is speeding up, not
slowing down. Whereas before, racial strife tended to
involve whites violently outlining their feelings about
blacks, the roles have become blurred: in 1976 for
example, the Notting Hill Carnival asserted Black
independence and Black mores. Increasingly too, race
has become identified with area and locality: names
like Brixton are now as distinctive as Chelsea or
Knightsbridge in other contexts, and the concentration
of Asians and West Indians has made inner city
constituencies a target for extremist political
agitation in recent by-elections.

The third change is by comparison prosaic:
simply the publication of the 1971 Census of Population.
However the analysis of the data by Professor John
Goddard and colleagues at the London School of Economics
underlined dramatically that society in Britain was
changing, not simply personally or economically, but
spatially as well.[6] Expressed simply, Goddard's
analysis showed that it is possible to split the city
into three components. The first is the core: the
city centre, and employment focus, which contains the
inner city. The second is the inner metropolitan
ring - a doughnut shaped area serving as the main
source of manpower for the core. Beyond this in turn
is an outer ring: the limit of commuting to any
particular core. When we compare the decades 1951-61,
and 1961-71, we find remarkable changes have taken
place, as Table One illustrates:

TABLE ONE: ABSOLUTE (OOO's) AND PERCENTAGE CHANGE,
WITHIN URBAN AREAS, 1951-71
(see text for details)

City Zone	1951-1961 absolute	%	1961-1971 absolute	%	
Cores	486	1.9	-729	-2.8	Population
	902	6.7	-439	-3.1	Employment
Rings	1721	13.3	2512	17.2	Population
	293	6.6	707	15.0	Employment
Outer	254	3.1	786	9.8	Population
Rings	-14	-0.4	130	3.9	Employment

(adapted from Goddard et al, 1976)

Most importantly, the core areas have lost both population
and employment - each has migrated to the inner, and to
some extent the outer rings. These aggregate figures
however hide some rather more startling changes. Table
Two outlines job losses from both core and inner rings
in the ten "worst" centres, and contrasts them with the
ten commuting areas where the largest absolute gains
have occurred.

TABLE TWO: MAJOR EMPLOYMENT GAINS AND LOSSES
FOR CORES AND INNER RINGS, 1961-71

Core and Inner Ring	Major Employment Loss 1961-71 (OOO's)	Core and Inner Ring	Major Employment Gain 1961-71 (OOO's)
London	-243.5	Portsmouth	32.1
Manchester	-84.2	Southampton	32.0
Glasgow	-59.7	Bristol	25.5
Liverpool	-34.1	Basildon	25.4
Leeds	-24.0	Oxford	25.1
Sheffield	-15.6	Ellesmere Port	22.1
Halifax	-7.8	Reading	19.7
Huddersfield	-6.8	Leicester	18.9
Kilmarnock	-6.3	Slough	18.3
Rhondda	-6.3	Basingstoke	18.1

(adapted from Goddard et al 1975)

Table Two shows that whilst some smaller centres, predominantly in the Southern counties, are still experiencing employment gain, others are experiencing net loss from both the core, and the surrounding inner ring. Of the larger centres, London is the worst case, with a loss of nearly one quarter of a million jobs. Behind we find the metropolitan areas of Manchester, Glasgow and Liverpool, Leeds and Sheffield, and with the exception of London, all the top ten centres experiencing loss are in the Assisted Areas. Clearly, the so-called "Regional Problem" has a part to play in this equation.[7]

From this discussion, we can see that Government interest in the so-called 'inner city crisis' is not a new phenomenon: instead the present debate simply reflects a change in strategy following a decade of area-based investment in housing, education and social services, to more economic issues (as we shall see in detail in the last Chapter). The efficacy of these past policies will be discussed below, but what seems clear is that the problems within the inner areas have in recent years been compounded by general economic, demographic and racial issues, thus producing a situation of far greater complexity, if not gravity. The basic problems are themselves however deep-seated, as Chapter Two outlines.

NOTES AND REFERENCES: CHAPTER ONE

1.   Foreword, to the Final Reports of the Inner Area Studies, HMSO, 1977.

2.   Peter Hall, "The inner cities dilemma", New Society, February 3, 1977.

3.   Peter Frankenberg, "Communities in Britain", Penguin Books, 1966.

4.   Richard Hoggart, "The uses of literacy", Penguin Books, 1958.

5. A very full history is provided by the National Community Development Project, "Gilding the ghetto", CDP, 1977.

6. This material is well summarised in the following papers: R. Drewett, J.G. Goddard, N. Spence, "Whats happening to British cities?", Town and Country Planning, 1975, 43, 12 pp. 523-30, and "Whats happening in British cities?", Town and Country Planning, 1976, 44, 1, pp. 14-24.

7. This point is elaborated upon by A.R. Townsend, "The relationship of inner city problems to regional policy", Regional Studies, 1977, 11, pp. 225-51.

Chapter Two

S O M E   D E F I N I T I O N S

INTRODUCTION

    Having discussed in general terms the policy
aspects of the inner city, it is now necessary to
introduce some definitions. Essentially, this chapter
deals with four questions. Firstly, how long has the
inner city existed as a particular problem? Secondly,
and perhaps most importantly, how does the so-called
crisis come about? Thirdly, whom does it effect, and
fourthly, where (within both the city and the country)
is the inner city problem to be found?

    Let us begin with the time factor.

A Temporal Perspective

    A speaker at a recent conference compared the
inner city conditions of the present with those
documented by Engels in Manchester in 1844.[1] Things
were a great deal worse then, suggested the speaker,
although the causes were the same; in a capitalist
society, there will always be those whose labour is
worth very little, and these unfortunates will always
gravitate toward the decaying cores where living is
cheapest. He continued to argue that such slums will
always be with us until capitalism itself disappears,
and little more than a continued cosmetic improvement
was likely to occur in the near future.[2]

    There is an element of truth in this statement,
but it overlooks one important point. In the nineteenth
century city, the homes of workers were clustered close
to their work. It was not until the advent of the
suburban railway that cities expanded, and this was
very much a twentieth century phenomenon. This is not

to suggest however that households were static. A
recent study of Leicester at the turn of the century
has shown that residents were extremely mobile, moving
from home to home with enormous regularity.[3]

Mobility has declined dramatically because of
the changes that have occurred within the housing market
since the first world war. In the early 1900's,
something like nine-tenths of all property was rented
from private landlords. Following the war, a grave
housing shortage precipitated the construction of the
first major developments of publicly-owned homes; this
sector now accounts for some 30% of all dwellings.
Equally, the suburban expansion that gave rise to
developments such as "Metroland" was speculative
investment based upon building for sale, not rent.[4]
Owner-occupation now accounts for something like 55%
of all homes, a figure that continues to grow.

The private rental market has shrunk apace and
with little renewal, it now contains a dwindling stock
of the oldest properties, frequently in the oldest parts
of the central areas of towns and cities. This means
that mobility is constrained in three ways. Firstly,
because those who rent from this sector live where
that accommodation is concentrated. Secondly, because
those who want local authority housing must show that
they need help, and must frequently wait for a home.
And thirdly, because those who want to buy property must
be able to obtain a mortgage.

This then is the major difference between the
nineteenth century city, and its contemporary counterpart.
The former had a populace living close to its industries
and machine-shops, living in appalling conditions
admittedly, but close to some sort of employment. The
modern city on the other hand, as we have seen, is
undergoing an out-movement of employment: *some workers
are however unable to migrate with the jobs.* They are

thus *"caught within what has been called the 'housing trap'. The choices available to them are owner-occupied houses, which they cannot buy, and public housing, to which they are denied access, and lacking the skills in greatest demand, they have been largely excluded from the new and expanding towns".*[5] It is in this sense that the inner city now contains an entirely different set of problems from that of a century ago.

The Housing Market: Who Gains, Who Loses?

Although we can identify a housing trap, it is by no means so easy to sketch those individuals and households who are caught.

As was intended, the DOE - sponsored consultants have produced a wealth of information about the inner areas of three of the largest conurbations. Particularly detailed data were collected by the team working in Lambeth; Table Three outlines the employment profiles of the households sampled in a study of Stockwell in 1973, and compares them with figures for the country as a whole, and for the Birmingham Inner Area of Small Heath.

TABLE THREE: COMPARISON OF PERCENTAGES OF HEADS OF HOUSEHOLDS IN EMPLOYMENT CATEGORIES, STOCKWELL, SMALL HEATH, AND GREAT BRITAIN

Employment	*Stockwell*	*Small Heath*	*Great Britain*
Professional and Managerial	10	4	18
Other Non-Manual	25	9	20
Skilled Manual	31	41	35
Semi-Skilled and Unskilled	34	46	27
TOTAL	100	100	100

(Source: Final Report, Lambeth Inner Area Study; Final Report, Birmingham Inner Area Study)

Most noticeably, there exist higher concentrations of
the poorly skilled, with compensatory losses in the
managerial category. These rather bald figures hide
the types of individuals involved though, and it may
be possible to flesh out this picture a little with
the use of some simple caricatures of inner-city
residents.

   a) The Elderly   Let us begin with those who
have lived in the areas the longest. They may remember
the neighbourhood as a stable working-class district;
a large proportion, perhaps a quarter, will have lived
in the same property since the war.[6] Many will live
alone; over two-thirds of the single-person families
in Liverpool are pensioners. They are fearful of the
changes taking place, and react most bitterly against
the coloured families - not necessarily because they
are black, but because of the latter's children, or in
the West Indians' case, because of a life-style that
is perceived to be noisy. Those not living in older
property may well be living in local authority tower-
blocks, where children are not easily catered for, and
where the elderly are used to fill vacant space.

   b) The Blacks   Although many whites have left
the core areas, blacks (a perhaps emotive term that is
nonetheless more accurate than the alternative
'immigrants'), have tended to move in the opposite
direction. This partly reflects their weakness in the
job market - due either to a lack of skills or
prejudice. West Indians are renters, and more usually
council tenants - over three-quarters fall into this
category nationally. Asians, in contrast, are strongly
attracted by owner-occupation. They operate however
within a twilight financial world, far removed from
the building societies. They buy cheaper, inner-city
properties within their price range, and in close
contact with their own communities. Research has shown

that Asians contradict the national trend by renting
when they are affluent, whilst in contrast the lower
socio-economic groups purchase more frequently.[7] This
does not mean though that the standard of property will
be in better condition than that in the rental sector.
Blacks have a higher representation in the unskilled and
poorly-skilled categories, and suffer higher unemployment.
Even in 1971, West Indian unemployment was running at
double the indigenous rate, a phenomenon that has also
been noted in the U.S.A. with respect to negro unemployment.
The concentration of ethnic groups into small communities
shows little sign of decreasing: the proportions have
risen to some 7% of the population of London as a whole,
and to 22% for an area like Stockwell.

c) The Professionals   Although they do not
account for a large proportion of residents, a notable
inclusion in the inner areas are young, relatively
affluent families who buy up poor quality housing as
an investment. Using local authority improvement
grants, perhaps obtained because the property is within
an HAA or a GIA, these households turn old dwellings
into very desirable ones. In some parts of Inner London,
the housing market has become geared to this process
of "gentrification", with estate agents and building
societies operating in close liason to attract such
buyers, at the expense of more traditional customers
like landlords.[8] Because of their life-style and
mores, antagonism between gentrifiers and longer-
standing residents can emerge, a friction noted some
years ago.[9] The more recent Lambeth study in contrast
notes some satisfaction that homes are being bought
and improved: the Inner Area Report concludes that
*"there seems to us much to be said for a continuing
process of gentrification in places like Stockwell."*[10]

d) The Rough   In a recent article about the
changing social climate, Dennis Marsden talked about

"the rough": that group that Marx called a
lumpenproletariat, and whom Sir Keith Joseph considered
were transmitting a culture of poverty to their
children.[11] It is clearly impossible to define such a
group, but there is a great deal of evidence to point
to a large number of individuals and households living
in various types of personal and practical stress. For
such people, employment, as we have seen, is becoming
increasingly hard to come by. As the skilled are
prepared to lower their job expectations to gain work,
it is left to the poorly-skilled to live on benefit.
In the Inner Area of Liverpool, unemployment was
running at 11.2% in 1971, compared with a national
average of 4.2%. In some core areas it rose as high
as 20%. However, with the deepening recession this
figure has risen to 17% in the Inner Area and a
staggering 30% in some neighbourhoods. The nature of
this unemployment was also particularly noticeable:
over half those unemployed had been so for at least
24 months out of the previous 60, whilst only a quarter
of those out of work are over 45 years of age, half the
national average.

     Other measures of stress can be, and have been
used. In Stockwell, the Lambeth team found that
approximately one in seven families were multiply
deprived, i.e. were suffering from three of the
following six measures of deprivation: low income,
overcrowding, lack of household amenities, lack of
car and telephone, disability and job instability.
In Small Heath, some 40% of households lived in
properties lacking all three basic amenities, (fixed
bath, exclusive use of W.C., and hot water). Other
signs of stress are less well-documented, but nonetheless
real: Lambeth recorded something like 500 incidences
of squatting in 1976 for example.

     These are clearly external measures of deprivation.

There is however also evidence for personal stress.
In some parts of Inner Liverpool, over one in six
families has only one parent. In Nottingham, a recent
study showed that concentrations of schizophrenia
were higher in the inner city than elsewhere in the
city, which the author attributed to the pressures of
the environment. Whilst there may be an element of
this, it is far more likely that the inability to hold
down a job, and the availability of the rooming or
lodging house in the core attracts such individuals.[12]
Returning to Liverpool once more, we may also draw
upon the results of a city-wide analysis of "social
malaise", which highlights the concentrations of
personal stress within particular parts of the housing
market. Webber's findings are that those living in
rooming houses and inner city council property display
heavy concentrations of stress in comparison to the city
average:

> *"The inner council estates for example suffer*
> *four times the average level of delinquency,*
> *three times the average youth job instability,*
> *supervision orders and school absenteeism and*
> *over twice the city-wide level of disinfestation,*
> *long term care, low reading ability, educational*
> *subnormality, free school meals, youth and long*
> *term unemployment. The only variables on which*
> *the (estates) experience lower concentrations...*
> *are illegitimacy, infectious diseases and children*
> *in care. These are the variables which are most*
> *highly concentrated in the rooming house area"*[13]

From these thumb-nail sketches, we can begin to
answer our question: who gains and who loses within
the housing market? Clearly, some gains are being
made: the gentrifiers for example, because of the
size and stability of their incomes, can attract
building society support. Others though cannot under-

take this sort of transaction: Asians particularly
have to borrow at frequently high rates of interest,
which restrict them to the cheapest properties.

The elderly too are losers: those who want to leave
the inner areas usually cannot; neither could they get
enough from the sale of their property to move to the
suburbs, nor could they take out a new mortgage. To
transfer to council property, even if such a move were
practically possible, could possibly also involve an
inner city tower block. In the main, inner area
council property has a reputation for containing
problem families as we have seen: either in so-called
deck-access blocks which have rapidly gone out of
fashion and are consequently difficult to let, or in
short-life clearance property and tenement buildings.

Nevertheless, to conclude this section it is
perhaps worthwhile quoting at length from the Liverpool
Inner Area Report.

> *"Studies have shown that in any deprived area*
> *only a minority is likely in any way to be*
> *deprived and that there are invariably more*
> *deprived people living outside deprived areas*
> *than within them...*
> *Successive generations living in deprived areas*
> *are faced with similar economic and social*
> *circumstances which in turn restrict their*
> *opportunities for advancement...many people*
> *living in such areas nevertheless maintain*
> *reasonable standards of behaviour, care for*
> *their home, and keep in employment".* [14]

Clearly, there is little to be gained from an attempt
to paint the inner areas as a seething sink of despair,
nor is there anything to be gained by overlooking the
deprivation that exists in some peripheral council
estates, mobile home parks, and many rural environments.
However, we should not ignore the fact that the inner

areas *do* possess a curious mixture of problems, in both a physical and human sense, and that even those in employment and in clean homes may not be enjoying a very satisfactory existence, as we shall see in Chapter Three.

A Spatial Perspective

Whilst we know a good deal about what happens in the inner city, we know a good deal less about *where* these problems are to be found, and this applies whether we are thinking about a particular city, or the country at large.

It may seem an unnecessary detail to want to draw lines about an area and to then call it the inner city; (as we have just seen, some suggest that there are plenty of "inner city problems" that are nowhere near the core areas, and that the drawing of lines is a futile exercise). However, there are two aspects to this problem. Firstly, we must relate any future policies to what we see to be the problems. However, the severity of these problems may be governed by where we look. If we take very small areas as the units likely to receive aid, then we can find pockets of very high unemployment, major deprivation, and so on. If we take larger areas, then the overall deprivation will be proportionaly less, as bad becomes balanced with not so bad. Clearly then, if government is to trim the policy cloth correctly, it needs to know just what sort of areas it is dealing with. This in turn leads on to the second consideration, for when aid is to be dispensed, it must go where it is needed. A simple observation perhaps, but as the Lambeth Report shows, the existing local government agency boundaries will not be adequate, because they tend to deal with different areas. A random selection of agencies who might be involved in any coordinated aid scheme, shows

that none share a responsibility for anything approaching
the same neighbourhoods; (examples include the Housing
Department, Social Services, the Health Services,
Supplementary Benefits, the Education Authority, the
Careers Service, the ward boundaries, the Probation
Officer, and so on).[15]

In fact, the most worrying aspect of the recent
Government policy initiatives, is that they are heavily
based upon three studies which have treated the problem
of area definition very differently. On Merseyside
for example, the Inner Area Study defined Inner Liverpool
as *"the total built up area of the city as it stood in
1921, when its population was 725,000. By 1971, the
population of the inner area had fallen to about
300,000 or just under half the total in the city"*.[16]
(Within this large area, a study area of approximately
60,000 inhabitants was also chosen; *"the main criterion
for its selection was that it should exhibit broadly
the range of inner area problems anticipated by the
consultants"*.[17] No statistics are however produced for
the smaller unit, and all the Report's conclusions are
based upon city-wide analyses).

In contrast, the Small Heath neighbourhood of
Birmingham was chosen for study because *"it was thought
to be about the right size, (falling in a preferred
population range of 30,000 to 40,000); had sharply
defined physical boundaries which, as subsequent
research confirmed, coincided closely with people's
'mental maps' of their district; presented a fairly
good mix of land-uses, housing and environmental
conditions, and tenure groups; was not scheduled for
large scale redevelopment beyond its western end; did
not have an 'abnormally high' proportion of immigrants,
(such as to make it totally atypical in terms of social
and racial mix); and had not been subject to major
previous research"*.[18]

Both these choices represent to rather varying
degrees, a certain set of assumptions about the types
of problem under investigation. They suggest (or are
at least consistent with the point of view) that there
exist such things as inner-city problems, and that
by setting up a small but representative "laboratory",
we can find out about them - how they happen, how they
can be solved. Such a stance is a direct result of
the DOE brief given to the consultants in 1972: the
teams were to

> *"discover by study a better definition of inner*
> *areas and their problems; investigate by*
> *experiments on the ground the actions affecting*
> *the physical environment of these areas which*
> *could usefully be undertaken for social*
> *environmental purposes".*

This reasoning is inadequate, for two apparently opposite
reasons. Firstly, it ignores the relationship between
social processes and *spatial problems*. For example,
just why is there a housing trap, and why does it
manifest itself in inner areas? Secondly, such a
standpoint assumes some sort of homogeneity within the
inner city, so that some areas can be thought representative.
But are all the pockets of deprivation similar? Are
areas of large, Victorian houses in multiple-occupation
really part of the same system of problems as run-down
council estates? As we have already seen, Liverpool's
city-wide statistical analysis did indeed suggest that
there existed such differences.

This point has also been examined thoughtfully
by the Lambeth team. They ask, *"to what extent could*
a relatively small area be representative of Inner
London as a whole?"[19] Their rhetorical question is
answered in the following manner; *"in debating this we*
found it helpful to pose two alternative approaches;
the 'strategic' and the 'tactical'". By strategic, they

mean the recognition that the study area's problems
were *"inextricably linked to dynamic processes at work
over the whole city and metropolitan region"*. Equally,
any policy suggestions emerging from the study area
would be recognised as being *"too specific, short term,
and palliative"*.In contrast, a tactical approach might
overcome the lack of pragmatism inherent in long-term
solutions, if only *"a properly handled analysis could
be generalised to other areas in the city"*. In the
final analysis, emphasis was placed upon the labour
market, and the changing socio-economic structure
within London which *"turned out to be amongst the
most important tackled"*.[20]

It would appear then that the process of choosing
the Inner Area bases may have made crucial assumptions
about the inner city. However, there is yet a further
dimension to this, in so far as the national perspective
must be considered. The three studies in question
have concentrated upon the major English conurbations.
Glasgow, with its distinctive housing problems and
concentrated malaise, has been overlooked. However,
more importantly, the whole stratum of second-order
cities with industrial decay has been passed over -
Leeds, Nottingham, Newcastle, Manchester. Furthermore,
an opportunity to investigate in depth the small centres,
such as Derby, Swansea and Hull has been missed.
Nonetheless, pointers exist that scaled-down problems
(in numbers, if not in gravity) exist: Reading for
example contains one Housing Action Area, and has
recently applied for a second declaration.

These variations, both spatial and in population
terms, may pose serious problems to any attempt to
create a unified strategy to policy implementation.
Some centres are in Development Areas, with all that
this entails for industrial assistance; London,
noticeably is not. Some centres have overall housing

shortages; others, for example those in the Northern region, have far less pressure upon the overall stock – although conditions may not be good, rent levels are nevertheless proportionately low. The industrial structure is as varied as each centre, in terms of the proportions of stable, declining or growth activities; equally the opportunities for women workers vary greatly. In the final analysis, these perceived variations may represent no problem to policy formulation; it is clearly a weakness however that this must remain as yet an assumption.

NOTES AND REFERENCES: CHAPTER TWO

1. F. Engels, "The condition of the working-class in England", Progress.

2. C. Paris, "Race in the inner city; the Government policy decisions", Paper presented to British Sociological Association Conference, London, December 1977.

3. R.M. Pritchard, "Housing and the spatial structure of the city", Cambridge University Press, 1976.

4. A.A. Jackson, "Semi detached London", G. Allen and Unwin, 1973.

5. Department of the Environment, "Inner area Studies", HMSO, 1977, p. 44.

6. A fact noted in a study of Newcastle-upon-Tyne by the author.

7. D. Smith, "The Disadvantages of racial minorities in housing", Paper presented to British Sociological Association Conference, London, December 1977.

8. J. Bugler, "Invaders of Islington", New Society, pp. 226-8, 1968.

9. P.W. Williams, "The role of institutions in the Inner London housing market: the case of Islington", Transactions, Institute of British Geographers, 1976, NS 1, 1, pp. 72-81.

10. Department of the Environment, "Inner London: policies for dispersal and balance", HMSO, 1977, p.34.

11. D. Marsden, "The rough", New Society, 11 November 1976, pp. 298-300.

12. J.A. Giggs, "The distribution of schizophrenics in Nottingham", Transactions, Institute of British Geographers, 1973, 59, pp. 55-76. The opposing view concerning the role of the housing market is given by G. Gudgin, "The distribution of schizophrenics in Nottingham - a comment", Transactions, Institute of British Geographers, 1975, 64, pp. 148-9.

13. R.J. Webber, "Liverpool Social Area Study 1971 Data: Final Report", PRAG Technical Papers TP14, 1975, Centre for Environmental Studies.

14. Department of the Environment, "Change or decay", HMSO, 1977, p. 96.

15. Department of the Environment, "Inner London", HMSO, 1977, p. 169.

16. Department of the Environment, "Inner area studies", HMSO, 1977, p. 4.

17. Department of the Environment, "Change or decay", HMSO, 1977, p. 13.

18. Department of the Environment, "Unequal city", HMSO, 1977, pp. 11, 12.

19. Department of the Environment, "Inner London", HMSO, 1977, p. 7.

20. Ibid, p. 8.

Chapter Three

THE COMPONENTS OF DECAY

INTRODUCTION

Chapters One and Two have attempted to come to
terms with some basic questions about the problems of
the inner areas, such as when?, and where? We can now
proceed to the finer detail of the subject, and consider
the practical implications of the inner city problem.
Accordingly, Chapter Three sets out the components
involved: employment, schooling, housing, medicine,
transport and retailing, discussing their organisation
and status. Chapter Four deals with an altogether
more contentious issue, namely the impacts and results
of their operation for inner city residents. We begin
with employment.

Industry, Employment and Population

It has recently been suggested that *"the essential
difference between the 1977 analysis of the urban
crisis and the previous versions is general agreement
that the central problem is economic: the rapid
decline of the economic base of the inner city. Other
evident problems need treatment too - housing, transport,
administration. But they need analysing, above all, in
terms of their effect on employment"*.[1]

I think that this is more than half true, but
unfortunately not completely correct. To begin with
it assumes that the economic question, which is generally
rationalised as unemployment, is a more serious issue
than the "quality of life". This I would dispute, and
will elaborate upon in the next chapter. Further,
there seems to be an implicit assumption here that
unemployment is a greater economic problem than large

concentrations of poorly skilled workers tied to poorly-paid precarious jobs; (nor should it be thought that concentrations of the lowly-skilled are a recent phenomenon). And finally, there is the assumption that any policy initiatives must rest primarily with the revitalisation of urban industry, to overcome this unemployment.

Let us begin with a sketch of the employment situation in the inner areas at the end of the fifties, before the out-migration of population and employment noted in Chapter One achieved particular momentum. Figures from London show that even at this date, an important proportion of the labour force was concentrated within the economically weakest sectors, namely the unskilled and semi-skilled; (by this we mean occupations like labouring, window cleaning or portering, and bus conducting or catering respectively).

TABLE FOUR: PROPORTIONS OF SEMI-SKILLED AND UNSKILLED
IN SECTORS OF LONDON, 1961

Occupational Group	Inner London	Middle Ring	Outer London
Semi-Skilled	16.5	15.6	12.5
Unskilled	11.8	9.1	5.5
All Groups	100.0	100.0	100.0

(Source: adapted from Lomas 1973)[2]

When we compare these figures with more recent data from 1971, we find only slight changes; (figures for Stockwell are included for comparison):

TABLE FIVE: PROPORTIONS OF SEMI-SKILLED AND UNSKILLED
IN SECTORS OF LONDON, 1961, 1971 and 1973

Occupational Group	Inner London 1961	Inner London 1971	Stockwell 1973
Semi-Skilled	16.5	17.5	22
Unskilled	11.8	1o.4	12

(Sources: Lomas 1973, Census of Population 1971, Inner London 1977)

This means that the proportions of the weakest socio-
economic groups have stayed very consistent. From this
we can infer two things: firstly that the inner-city
poor have been there for some time, and secondly that
the out-migration of labour and jobs does not seem to
have produced a proportionate increase of major dimensions
in the numbers of the poorly-skilled in the inner areas;
(the figures for the other conurbations do not reveal a
trend significantly different from that of London).

What sort of employment, and what sort of people
have left then; where have they gone, and what has
brought this change about?

Firstly, we should make it clear that the people
who moved went before the jobs: in the 1960's, *"at
the aggregate national scale, the decentralization of
population was leading the decentralization of jobs".*[3]
In part, this movement was a reflection of economic
necessity within the housing market; simply those
wanting owner-occupied housing have perceived the best
investments to be in the suburbs, a point discussed
further below. In part, it was a rejection of the
urban lifestyle, in preference for a *sub-urban* habitat.
This again emerges in the section on Housing in this
chapter.

What this centrifugal movement does *not* reflect is a movement of households from the inner cities to the New Towns. The recent juxtaposition by Peter Shore of an announcement designed to curtail New Town investment, and to initiate an 'Inner City strategy', seemed to suggest that government has identified such a causal connection. It would seem that reduced growth within the New and Expanded Towns is designed to slow down the out-migration of people from nearby towns and cities. However, there is no evidence that such major migrations have occurred. For example, of movements to one of the more recent New Towns, that of Central Lancashire, only 4.7% of families came from Merseyside, and 7.6% from Greater Manchester. In contrast, 6.7% of families moved from the South-East, and 6.4% from overseas.[4] These statistics may be compared with the proportions of migrants nominated by the GLC for properties in the New and Expanding towns; approximately 8% of those leaving London in the 1960's were involved in this type of planned move.[5]

If population has voted with its feet with respect to the conurbations and larger cities, what has happened to the employment situation? Essentially, two factors are involved here: the *closure* of urban industry, and the *migration* of some types of activity.

From London once more, we have evidence that a large proportion of the industrial enterprises which disappear also cease to trade. In the South-East London labour area, for example, 74% of the firms closing between 1970-1975 did so as a result of winding up their activities.[6] This seems to be a general trend, operating right across all types of activity, and all sizes of establishment. When we seek for explanations, a spectrum offers itself. Gripaios suggests that "*the fact that there were closures in virtually all industry orders indicates that locational factors have been responsible for decline in the South London Area".*[7] This is partly true. Some firms that move, as we shall see, require facilities that such areas cannot give. However, there is also the structural question. Simply, many inner city activities fold, either because they are producing, or are related to, obsolete goods, or often because they are ephemeral activities in the first place: using cheap, near-derelict premises for a few months at a time to make skate-boards or supply mail-order goods.

Of course, firm closures are only a part of the story. Job loss from existing firms and services continues unabated. Small Heath, in Birmingham, has experienced a 39% loss of jobs in the last 15 years. Barbara Smith provides several detailed examples: for instance, the loss of 100 jobs for conductors following a move to one-man buses at a local authority bus garage. Once more, those with skills keep their employment at the expense of the less skilled. On a larger scale, there is the long-term loss of nearby 4000 jobs from the B.S.A. engineering concern. The first jobs were lost with the decline of the cycle trade in the 1960's, whilst over two thousand were made redundant in 1976 following the collapse of motor-cycle production. This latter example underlines the structural factor, with an enterprise unable to come to terms with changing tastes: firstly, the falling demand for cycles as car-ownership increased, and secondly the competition from Japanese and Italian competitors in the motor-cycle sector.[8]

In other areas, the dependence upon declining sectors has followed a different route to the same destination. In Liverpool for example, a traditional source of inner area employment has been not skilled engineering, but casual manual labour in the docks:

in 1950. 14% of all Merseyside's employment was in the
docks, with another 21% involved in related activities
like warehousing and handling. In 1973, these
proportions had sunk to 5% and 13% respectively. Other
jobs based on the role of the port also seem precarious;
"Tate and Lyle, whose vast bulk overshadows all, and
in which several thousand workers are employed, has
been threatening to pull out for years". [9] In such
contexts, the relationships between the urban problem
and the regional problem become blurred - the
continuing decline of traditional activities like
shipbuilding on the Clyde and the Tyne is not simply a
product of changes at the city scale, for example.

   When we consider the employment situation in
terms such as the long-term running-down of certain
activities, it becomes very difficult to relate the
problem back to any practical remedies. Things are
however not so bleak in relation to the *movements* of
firms: at least in this case it is possible to find
out why many concerns are leaving the inner areas.

   It will be remembered that in the South-East
London example, approximately one quarter of firms were
physically transferring their activities to another
site. These tended to be the larger, manufacturing
concerns, as opposed for example to services which
seem to wither away as their supporting activities,
like manufacturing, leave or die. The destinations of
the moves are perhaps surprising, indicating that the
New Towns are once more *not* scape-goats.

TABLE SIX: DESTINATIONS OF ESTABLISHMENTS LEAVING
SOUTH-EAST LONDON, 1970-5

Destination	Proportion of Relocations
South-East London	35.9%
Elsewhere within Inner London	12.0%
Outer London	6.5%
Outer Metropolitan Area	15.2%
Elsewhere in the South-East	16.3%
New Towns	2.1%
Development Areas	3.3%
Others	8.7%

(Source: P. Gripaios, 1977)

As Table Six shows, very little movement is in
the nature of a long migration. The average distance
travelled from the old to a new site is approximately
26 miles: from the areas away from the very heart
of London (e.g. Woolwich), the distance falls to
single figures.[10] Such information seems to cast
doubt upon the accepted notions that spacious greenfield sites are highly-prized by all firms. Indeed,
of 180 firms studied by Barbara Smith in Birmingham,
which moved within the conurbation, 56% were forced to
move due to redevelopment or the loss of a lease.
Similarly, of 115 moves within the wider West Midlands
region, 36% were caused by take-overs and rationalisation
thereafter.[11] Whilst nearly half the firms in the
regional-mover category did give space requirements as
a reason for moving, it is clear that as far as future
policies are concerned, it is not simply a question of
the new industrial sites enticing firms away from the
inner city, which must be remedied. On the other side
of the coin however, it must be recognised that
these remarks do not apply to the locational decisions

of new firms, either spontaneously coming into being,
or moving from other regions. Here the suburban
trading-estate or overspill area has a major advantage,
as the growth in centres like Luton, Kirby, Telford or
Washington testifies.

To conclude this section, it is perhaps worthwhile
mentioning one further dimension of the industrial
situation. There is some evidence that a certain
degree of bouyancy exists in the sector of small
businesses run by Asian entrepreneurs, and that the
immigrant community is actively investing within the
inner city. There is however also evidence that
conditions within these firms may not be very high:
poor pay and long hours seem typical of enterprises
which involve many machine-shops producing garments,
but are also found in larger establishments, of which
Grunwicks, the photographic concern, is best known.
This seems an almost inevitable by-product of bringing
employment to the inner areas, and one which is discussed
in relation to policy formulation in Chapter Five.

Housing

This section on housing is a long one, not only
because the problems relating to housing within the
inner areas are extensive, but also because they are
central to the individual who lives in the inner city.
They are central because the home acts as a basic
insulation between that individual and his environment.
After all, unemployment can be ameliorated by social
security payments, although these make it no less
problematic. Housing conditions on the other hand
are not easily improved; nor can a poor home environment
easily be compensated for. Overcrowding, damp, vermin
and cold can all interact to destroy the ability of
any family to cope with the basics of life.

In a recent analysis of housing within the inner

city, seven problems were identified as being in need
of solution. These are as follows:

a)   large numbers of houses without basic amenities;
b)   a deteriorating state of repair of houses;
c)   a declining supply of unfurnished rented property;
d)   shortage of furnished rented accommodation,
      particularly for young single people and those
      in need of extra care;
e)   a congested and unattractive physical environment;
f)   a growing number of low income owner-occupiers
      experiencing difficulty in obtaining mortgages;
g)   lack of public and private investment in new
      housing or in mortgage lending on existing
      housing. [12]

Let us begin with the basic factual information. In
Liverpool, the following numbers of households were
without the most basic amenities in 1971: 32,000
lacked exclusive use of hot water (16% of all households);
46,000 (23%) lacked exclusive use of a bath; and 58,000
(30%) lacked exclusive use of an inside W.C. On
Tyneside, as many as 69% of households in some wards
lacked an inside toilet: a similar proportion of
properties were without a fixed bath in 1971. [13] A
large-scale statistical analysis of all the small-area
census districts in Great Britain, undertaken by the
DOE, has shown remarkable concentrations of housing
stress in some conurbations. For example, in some
4378 enumeration districts (EDs), over 70% of households
are without exclusive use of these basic amenities:
950 of these EDs are concentrated within inner London. [14]

        Coupled with this lack of facilities is the state
of the housing stock, which is indeed deteriorating.
In Liverpool once more, typical with its large
concentrations of Victorian properties, an astonishing
62,000 dwellings are thought to be in need of improvement:

33,000 of these require "urgent action" in the opinion
of the Housing Department. This becomes more understand-
able if it is realised that 82,000 dwellings, over one-
third of the city's total stock, were built pre-1919.

Why is the stock within the core areas in such
poor condition? The age factor has already been cited.
More important however is the failure of government
legislation, designed to improve homes, to make any
sort of major impact upon the conditions of the
majority of properties. It will be remembered from
Chapter One that two major items of legislation exist
to provide funds for this type of improvement - the
end product of these Acts are the GIAs and HAAs. GIAs
are typically found in smaller towns and cities, where
concentrations of housing stress are less noticeable.
From one such local authority however, there is
evidence that the aims of the 1969 Housing Act, coupled
with local attitudes, tend to work against the
requirements of stress neighbourhoods. In a study of
Huddersfield, it was noted that some 36 neighbourhoods
were chosen for possible GIA declaration, excluding to
begin with areas where rateable values were higher
than the statutory maximum.[15] A secondary analysis of
areas in need then concentrated upon the removal of
neighbourhoods where large concentrations of elderly
families or immigrant households were to be found.
Although such a choice was not inconsistent with the
intentions of the 1969 Act, Duncan observed a tendency
to concentrate upon prestigious projects which would
reflect well upon the authority, rather than any
particular commitment to the principle of improvement.

HAAs, on the other hand, are specifically designed
to be declared within neighbourhoods where housing and
social stress are more apparent. The number of HAAs
remains however very small (only 168 declarations
within 59 districts in the first two years, 1975-77),

and the number of homes scheduled for improvement is similarly disappointing, (approximately 60,000 in England, out of a potential 700,000).[16] Once more the distribution of declarations is very uneven: Scotland for example has little planned improvement despite its major housing problems. The majority of HAAs are within the conurbations, although even here, the distributions are skewed. In London for example, outer Boroughs like Bromley possess a Housing Action Area, whilst inner Boroughs like Tower Hamlets and Camden do not. Just why this should be is puzzling. Indeed, when we look at housing strategies in the widest contexts, we find some Boroughs pursuing very vigorous policies across the board, and others virtually quiescent, despite very similar problems. Boroughs like Islington, for example, have high rates of HAA declaration, new building, and clearance, whilst others, like Tower Hamlets, show limited activity in any sphere. Curiously, this does not seem to relate to party politics; Boroughs like Kensington and Chelsea with Conservative councils have HAA declarations, whilst Labour ones have not.[17]

Unfortunately, the declaration of areas for improvement is only half the story. Once done, there still remains the task of convincing landlords or homeowners that the cost of improvement is worthwhile. Homeowners, (and approximately half the dwellings in HAAs and GIAs are so owned) may gain financial assistance only up to the £5,000 mark: and yet many basic conversions such as the addition of a bathroom can cost well above this figure. Landlords are similarly sceptical, for although the returns on property are fairly poor in the main, the market is continually contracting, whilst demand remains constant. There is thus no question of trying to attract tenants. On the other side of the coin however, an improvement

cannot be followed by a wholesale increase in rents;
nor can the property be sold within the following five
years.[18] In short, the whole question of improvement
is extremely problematic, and opinion still divides on
the possibility of success.[19]

The wider issue of finance is clearly central to
the inner city housing market, and manifests itself
within all three sectors. Landlords, as I have
suggested, get little return from their property. In
the main this has little to do with the existence of
the numerous Rent Acts, and is more the result of the
financial situation of those who use rented accommodation.
Even with rent rebates available, demand for housing is
very elastic: in other words, rent incrases tend to
result in overcrowding, and multiple-occupation, (rent
rebates also have ceilings, and cannot cover rents
that are not "fair"). In the final analysis we come
down to the basic question that if tenants could afford
high rents, then many might be able to purchase
property, and in turn qualify for the extensive subsidies
available for home owners. (The recently published
Green Paper on housing shows that the average house
buyer receives £141 per annum in mortgage relief: this
compares with the £139 per annum subsidy on the average
council rental. The private tenant receives no formal
subsidy as such).[20]

As a result of the financial situation within the
market, landlords tend to be small businessmen. A
study in London shows that *"almost all the landlords
of furnished dwellings referred to the Rent Tribunal
were private individuals holding only one house and
having occupations other than managing their property"*.[21]
Because of their limited means, they cannot maintain
their property in the way that older property
particularly requires.

The precarious state of landlordism suggest that

other financial forces are required in the inner areas.
Building Society funds, which might enable tenants or
new movers to buy previously rented dwellings, are
however very scarce within the core area. A study in
Newcastle-upon-Tyne shows that some districts are
entirely overlooked by Building Society Association
(BSA) funds,[22] usually on the grounds of the age of the
property. It is in fact commonly assumed that many
BSA members operate a system of *red-lining*, whereby
certain inner city districts are regarded as 'off-limits'
to investment. In defence, these policies could be
regarded as attempts to safeguard investors' interests,
by not lending on property which could lose value in
the wake of re-development proposals for example. The
net result however is very much a self-fulfilling
prophecy.

B/- Soc s
red-lining

If we look at alternative sources of finance, we
tend to find that local authorities have been prepared
to grant mortgages on inner area property: indeed the
study of Boddy suggested that BSA funds and local
authority funds cater for entirely different parts of
the city.[23] Paradoxically, public funds tend to be
offered over shorter terms, at higher rates of interest,
and frequently on a smaller percentage of the selling
price than commercial mortgages: high rates of refusal
are common, suggests research in Bristol, since
prospective purchasers cannot afford the necessary
deposit and repayments.[24] Furthermore, local authority
funds are still severely constrained: in Liverpool
for example, the total municipal allocation of mortgage
funds for 1977-8 works out as a ratio of £9.35 per
1000 households.

Local authorities are of course also represented
as landlords within the inner city with large numbers
of council properties. These cover a wide range of
properties, from compulsorily-purchased dwellings in

clearance areas used for temporary accommodation,
through to enormous tower blocks on redevelopment
estates. In the main however, many of these properties
are unpopular, either because of the age, or the
condition, or the design. This is especially true of
the many types of flats, which are particularly prone
to vandalism and neglect, a point discussed with some
sensitivity by the Lambeth Inner Area Study.[25] As we
shall see in Chapter Four, the local authority housing
departments have payed the penalty for playing what
Valerie Karn has called 'the numbers game': trying to
clear, and rebuild quickly, in order to rehouse as
many people as possible.

From these remarks, it is possible to generalise
that the financial situation is currently doing more
to damage the inner city than to aid it. The lack of
what the Housing Green Paper calls "general assistance"
to private tenants, the costs of local authority
mortgages, and the regressive nature of tax support on
BSA loans (whereby subsidies actually increase with
income) all work against any improvement in the inner
city housing market. Only in one sector is growth
actually taking place, that of Housing Associations.
Through the media of the Housing Corporation and the
DOE, some 13,800 properties will be rehabilitated in
Great Britain in 1977-8. Whilst some Associations
are quite small, others are becoming major property
owners, and are taking up much of the slack left by
landlords selling out. More importantly, money is
available to finance new-build schemes, many of which
specifically cater for the minority groups mentioned
in Chapter Two. Whilst some Associations specialise
in the building of 'sheltered units' for old people,
(small blocks of flats with communal facilities and
some supervision), others concentrate upon single-
parent families. Some Associations too have had the

flexibility to cope with rather special cases, such as
the influx of Ugandan Asians, and latterly Chilean
refugees. For all this however Housing Associations
are the cause of some disquiet: they have been termed
"the new slum landlords", for example, and are not
answerable to local communities in the way that local
authority housing departments are nominally controlled.
These questions of access and control are taken up
more fully in Chapter Four.

Medicine and the Social Services

One of the recurring themes throughout this work
is the notion that inner city residents are in some
sort of stress; indeed, the Final Reports of the Inner
Area studies are liberally peppered with quotes from
residents who complain of ill-health brought about by
the general environment. Moreover, many of the
residents are elderly, or without a marriage partner,
or have larger than average families.

In response to these needs, we should expect a
concentration of social services designed to cope with
such problems - medical practitioners, welfare workers,
clinics, and so on. When we come to investigate the
situation, it is difficult however to find any hard
information on the inner city supply of such resources.

As far as the U.S.A. is concerned, there exists
a great deal of evidence that inner city ghettoes
possess very poor social services. Indeed a series of
studies have shown that negroes tend to have to use
the central hospitals for minor ailments, as doctors
are so few. Because of this, their journeys for
treatment are long and expensive, and perhaps in some
cases also potentially injurious. Furthermore,
medical treatment tends to become remedial, rather
than preventive, which also of course increases the
risks.[26]

There is in contrast little information about British cities, a situation that the growth of Area Health Authorities has done nothing to change: most comparative statistics are at the regional scale. We may thus turn to the Inner Area studies for detailed information about these types of resources.

One of the most interesting documents available relates to an "Area Resource Analysis" of a small part of the Liverpool inner city, known as 'Liverpool D'. The area contains 9.6% of the city population, 9% of the retired population, and 8.9% of the school-age children. The study found that *"9.3% of the social services expenditure that was not allocated purely on the basis of population went to District D"*,[27] (in other words, both the per capita and non-per capita provision was apparently equitable). Quite large proportions of children from District D were in care, whilst quite high percentages of elderly people were in local authority or voluntary homes. In general *"the picture that emerges of the social services is of little or no overall discrimination for or against District D"*.[28]

Lamentably, this one analysis is all we have to draw upon. As the Liverpool team reports, when they began their investigation, *"such information did not exist. Moreover, nobody had thought to ask"*.[29] This is a highly revealing remark, and one that highlights a point that I have already introduced: namely, the mistaken view that the inner city problem can be seen simply as an economic problem (the loss of jobs) or a housing problem (the housing trap). The *quality of life* does not seem to have been seriously examined. We do not seem to have the basic data to tell us first of all if the resources that are provided for the inner areas are up to their role, and secondly what the impacts of this provision are.

Interestingly, both the Lambeth and Birmingham reports deal not with the quantity and quality of facilities and resources, but rather with the organisation of welfare delivery. One factor already mentioned is the boundary problem, which means that households do not know where to go to get advice or help. In Stockwell, the following 'non-take-up' of benefits was found amongst families where the total income was less than 120% of that possible on supplementary benefit:

TABLE SEVEN: HOUSEHOLDS BELOW POVERTY LINE,
AND UPTAKE OF VARIOUS BENEFITS

Household	Proportion not Receiving Benefit
Head not working: not receiving supplementary benefit	37%
Households without rate rebates	82%
Council tenants without rate rebates	40%
Unfurnished tenants without rent allowances	83%

(Source: Inner London, 1977, p. 145)

Such a low take-up of aid clearly suggests that communications are poor, (or far less likely, that households are loath to accept state assistance). This point is underlined by the Small Heath study which shows how important very simple links may be. They show how valuable an Asian language speaking welfare officer was in attracting mothers to bring their children to nurseries for example.

Nonetheless, these reports have failed to come to terms with the basic question of the relationships between the existence, not of the 'universal' resources

like supplementary benefit, but those found only in
specific locations, and deprivation caused by their
absence. As Peter Ambrose has recently pointed out,
there are three components to the question of
"effective accessibility". In relation to a facility
like a medical centre, we must consider the time spent
travelling to the centre from home, the cost of the
journey, and the time spent waiting within the centre.
In a sense, all three have spatial overtones: the
first two relate to the location of the clinic - is
it where it should be? The third is also spatial in
the sense that queuing is a measure of provision - in
other words are the resources sufficient for that
particular location, or should more be transferred
from other parts of the city or region?[30]

Evidence that the distribution of resources may
have major impacts upon those individuals who are
poorly served is provided by an analysis undertaken
by geographers in Newcastle-upon-Tyne. We noted that
some parts of the city are very poorly served by
dentists, whilst others are very well provided for.
This is especially the case for the higher status
parts of the city, where many N.H.S. dentists are
concentrated. In contrast, the inner city and local
authority housing areas are served by the dental
clinics attached to medical centres. When we came to
examine the dental health of schoolchildren within
the Area Health Authority, we found that children from
areas where working-class households predominated had
a higher incidence of dental ill-health than children
from middle-class areas. This has been noted before,
and usually attributed to attitudinal factors such as
poor dental hygiene. However, there also existed a
stronger correlation between the rate of dental decay
in a neighbourhood, and the ease of visiting the local
N.H.S. practitioner. These areas lacking immediate

proximity to a dentist appear not to use the clinic service, and to consequently neglect treatment.[31]

As we shall see in Chapter Four, the relationships between service provision and the incidence of what we may call 'social malaise' are by no means simple. Whilst a lack of provision may affect health, it cannot be assumed that, say, a shortage of police officers will automatically result in a rise in crime rates. Equally, as we shall see in the case of school provision and educational attainment it is difficult to measure the importance of the home background: the extent to which parents themselves limit children's ability to exploit teaching resources to the full, for example. A third problem relates to the siting of facilities with respect to the user population. A study of family planning clinics in London for instance has recently shown that in relation to the proportions of 'women at risk', the London boroughs that constitute the Inner London Education Authority are *"well-provided with clinics, and that in all the measures adopted here (are) better placed than Outer London"*.[32] Astonishingly, the study does not then relate provision to the rate of live births, in an attempt to relate provision with any concept of 'need'. Certainly, if births are not lower than elsewhere, this could suggest that the population does not want contraceptive advice, or is unwilling to use the facilities (the home influence at work). It could however also suggest, as the authors themselves opine, that *"Outer London residents make extensive use of the Inner London facilities, for many women go to a clinic close to their place of work which is more convenient for them than the clinic closest to their home address"*.[33] In other words, it is possible that the provision for inner area residents is relatively poor, because they provide for the whole of London, potentially, and not simply the local population 'at risk'.

Such problems are central to an assessment of the quality of inner city life. As Ray Pahl the sociologist has observed, *"a systematic sociology of public provision has hardly started, despite the contention of one urban economist that local public services bid fair to become the chief means of income redistribution in our economy."*[34]

As he continues, however, *"only educational provision has been systematically studied"*,[35] and it is to this that we now turn.

Education

The provision of educational services deserves separate treatment, partly because it relates so directly to the job market, with all that this entails for social and thus spatial mobility, and partly because it has received major Government attention within the inner areas.

The landmark within this history is the 1967 Plowden Report, which noted a relationship between family and social deprivation on the one hand, and poor educational attainment on the other. Of importance within Plowden was the emphasis placed upon the primary school, in attempting to break this cycle of parental poverty, poor educational attainment, and the possession of low job skills by successive generations. As Herbert rightly points out, this does not mean that poor achievement was assumed to pass from parents to children, (the so-called culture of poverty thesis); rather the emphasis within Plowden was upon the ability of schools to cope with the demands placed upon them.

"We have ourselves seen schools caught in such vicious circles...they are quite untypical of schools in the rest of the country...tiny

> *playgrounds; gaunt looking buildings; often*
> *poor decorative conditions inside; narrow*
> *passages; dark rooms; unheated and cramped*
> *cloakrooms; unroofed outside lavatories; tiny*
> *staff rooms; inadequate storage space with*
> *consequent restriction on teaching material and*
> *therefore methods; inadequate space for movement*
> *and PT; meals in classrooms; art on desks; music*
> *only to the discomfort of others in an echoing*
> *building; non-sound proof partitions between*
> *classes; lack of smaller rooms for group work...*
> *and, sometimes all around, the ingrained grime*
> *of generations."*[36]

This has been rendered a good deal more bluntly in the
description of *"slum schools"*.[37]

From this initial investigation emerged the
Educational Priority Areas (EPAs) already introduced
in Chapter One. In 1968, a joint strategy was
financed by the Department of Education and Science and
the Social Science Research Council to set up five
action projects, designed both to research the problems
of inner area schools, and to investigate ameliorative
measures. The EPAs were established in Deptford,
Sparkbrook, Conisborough, Liverpool 8 and Dundee. A
spectrum of catchment area problems were used to define
the schools chosen:

TABLE EIGHT: CRITERIA FOR EPA CHOICE

Plowden Criteria	*Examples*
Social Class Characteristics	High proportions of fathers in social classes 4,5
Family Size	Four or more children in full time education
Supplements From the State	Infants receiving free school meals
Domestic Overcrowding and Sharing	Densities greater than 1.5 persons per room
Poor School Attendance	New school entrants absent without explanation
Disturbed and Handicapped Pupils	Children with brother/sister attending special or remedial class
Incomplete Families	Mother or father absent
Children Unable to Speak English	Mother-tongue other than English

Adapted from Ferguson et al, 1971 [38]

The scale of the problems within some catchments may be shown by the index produced by the Inner London Education Authority. By scaling the types of variables outlined in Table Eight, they were able to rank the school catchments. In the school emerging as most problematic, *"nearly half of the employed men in the immediate area were in semi-skilled or unskilled jobs, half of the children in the area were in large families, one-eighth of the households in the area were technically overcrowded and over one-third of them were without inside lavatories. Nearly one-third of the children received free school dinners, an average of one-seventh of the children were absent in a selected week,.two-thirds of the children were immigrants, three-quarters of them were placed in the lowest quartile on an ability test. Over half of them had an incomplete year at the school and four out of five teachers had been there for less than three years."*[39]

The initial EPA schemes have been added to, with schools in need receiving preferential treatment with respect to teachers' salaries (to try to slow down staff turnovers) and building grants. Over time, a shift of emphasis has also emerged with respect to curriculum development, resulting in a re-assessment of early post-war attitudes which foresaw different educational needs for different groups: (this in turn resulted in grammar and secondary modern schools). The Liverpool Inner Area Study for example *"concluded that in EPA schools the balance of curriculum should change from academic to social, be based upon the immediate environment, and that there should be an increase in the time spent upon creative pursuits involving the parents"*.[40] This brings us firmly up against the relationships between inputs and attainment, about which there exists an enormous literature: an attempt is made to synthesise this material in the section 'Education & Attainment' in Chapter Four.

So far this section has concentrated upon the primary, or most locally-based school within the inner areas. As we have seen, many of these are old, outmoded, and yet must cater for especially needy children. What however of the secondary education situation?

Two studies suggest themselves for further analysis. The first examined provision of resources to various comprehensive schools, on the basis of the proportions of middle, or working-class children in attendance. This study noted that in schools with large proportions of working-class children, there was greater expenditure upon teaching materials, and that better teacher-pupil

ratios existed; (despite this, attainment was lower
than in schools where lower proportions of working-
class children were found, and less resources were
spent).[41] Whilst this research does not specifically
involve an inner city consideration, the second analysis
has a clear geographical component. In another study
of Newcastle-upon-Tyne, the catchments of the nine
comprehensives in the city were examined. It was found
that for one school, six of its seven assigned feeder
primaries are in EPAs, producing a heavy concentration
of children from households in the poorest socio-
economic groups. This organisation followed a previous
situation, in which four inner city primaries sent
their children on to a comprehensive almost on the city
boundary, which involved the children travelling past
another comprehensive.[42] Nor was the concentration
matched by a concomitant allocation of educational
resources; three comprehensives with strong concentrations
of children from owner-occupied, high-status neighbourhoods
enjoyed an allocation of resources that were received
later by other schools, following periods of years in
some instances.

The question of resources supplied to schools
presents a suitable note upon which to conclude this
section, because there is little suggestion that the
EPA strategy has resulted in any major improvement in
the flow of funds to inner city schools. Indeed, matters
may well be still getting worse. The CDP reports that
Liverpool has not built a nursery school since 1969,
and as inner area populations decline, teachers are
also removed, through local authority spending cuts:
"your children are more likely to die in infancy, or
when, after getting no nursery schooling, they finally
get to school, of being in larger classes in worse
buildings".[43]

Transport

Whilst there is little to be found within the Inner
Area Studies Reports concerning the Social Services,
there is next to nothing to be learned concerning
transport provision and mobility. This does not
represent a national disinterest, for although Britain
has never come to terms with planning for the motor car,
it is very advanced in some areas: in real terms for
example, more was spent on the Roskill Commission's
Inquiry into the Third London Airport than on the
Inner Areas research, in total. Equally, some aspects
of transport deprivation are topical: the case of
rural areas springs readily to mind.

Intuitively, it is not obvious that inner city
residents should have transport problems, for if
commuters living in suburban areas can have access to
jobs in the central areas, why cannot those living close
to the city centres undertake the same journey in
reverse, out to suburban trading estates?

The answer lies of course with the modes of
transport on offer. The commuter is a great deal more
likely to own a car than his inner city counterpart;
this reflects both the economic status of the former,
which allows him to live in suburbia in the first
instance, and also a division in terms of job types:
the semi-skilled and unskilled are rarely offered the
private use of a vehicle as part of their employment.
When we come to look at the spatial variations of car
ownership, the differences are strikingly uniform.
In Tyne-Wear in 1971, for example, the majority of
inner areas had wards where between 75 and 88 per cent
of households lacked a car. In suburban districts,
the proportions range from one quarter to one half of
all households.[44]

In Liverpool, "car ownership in the inner areas is
only two-thirds of that in the city, dropping to less

56

than a quarter of the average in the inner council estates".[45] In Stockwell, as a reflection of wider regional disparities, approximately one third of households possess a car: in relative terms of course this is still below the general level of ownership, and furthermore, only fourteen per cent of workers use a car for work trips.

It is no exaggeration to suggest that most British cities are geared to an inflow, rather than an outflow of travellers every morning and evening. As if with some sort of ironical intent urban motorways have been built at the expense of the non-car user: in Gateshead for example, a part of the A1 was directed straight through the middle of an inner city council estate. The environmental impact was so great that finally some seventy properties were demolished. Only 12 per cent of households living on the estate possessed a car.[46]

For an outward journey, the inner city worker is reliant upon public transport. This is not a hardship necessarily in London; here the choice of modes is wider than in other large conurbations, where there are no underground systems, and where many local stations have been closed. The shining exception to this story is the Tyne-Wear Metro, a long-term project designed to link up the existing suburban railway with a new central underground system in Newcastle. For economy however the links will still emphasise suburban-centre moves; there will be no connection out to the west of the conurbation (where a large number of local authority estates with low car-ownership rates exist), and no connections out to the large industrial estates and new townships at Washington, Killingworth or the Team Valley.

The problem with relating the transport situation to personal mobility is the interpretation placed upon travel data. For example, in Liverpool, 50 per cent of

work trips utilised buses, and 23 per cent involved
walking. For some estates, the latter figure rose to
over a third. However, to what extent does walking to
work reflect local job opportunities, and to what
extent an unwillingness to travel for longer periods
of time, and at greater expense? The Liverpool study
shows that it would cost an inner area worker £5 a
week to travel to Ellesmere Port, £4.40 to Runcorn,
and £2.80 to Ford's at Halewood. More significantly,
each journey would take up between eighty and one
hundred and twenty minutes a day, figures that would
probably lengthen if the journey involved travel at
unsocial hours for shift-work. The study concludes that
"the boundaries of Liverpool can be taken as the effective
travel to work limit for residents of inner Liverpool. To
take up jobs further away means either having the use of
a car, or being prepared to move home"[47]: (to this we
might add the postscript, "or able to move home").

Retailing

So far the emphasis has been upon the provision of
public services, like education; there is however one
area of private provision of importance within any
community, and that is the number and quality of shops.

Inner city areas have always had an unusual
mixture of retailing outlets to draw upon. Frequently
within reach is the city centre, often still possessing
open-air markets. In addition is the once-ubiquitous
corner-shop, offering virtually every requirement in
the smallest possible amounts. In the last decade
however a continuing process of "rationalisation"
has served to change much of the basic structure of
retailing, especially as it relates to day-to-day
needs. Corner-shops have closed as populations have
disappeared. More importantly, central areas have
been in competition for investment with suburban

precincts, and around many Northern cities, out-of-town
shopping centres. In both instances, emphasis is upon
bulk-buying, linked to shopping trips based upon car
travel. In neither sense is the inner city shopper
catered for. A recent study has argued that redevelopment
is having a major impact upon inner areas second only
to job losses:

> *"throughout Inner London the number of*
> *neighbourhood shops is on the decline, but the*
> *rate of decline is most severe where*
> *redevelopment is taking place and where rents*
> *are going up. The new shops are inevitably*
> *expensive, of a different character unless the*
> *local authority subsidizes shopkeepers through*
> *low rents. The general pattern of shopping*
> *changes from a scatter of small shops to the*
> *concentration of shops in selected parades and*
> *in large regional centres. This suits the*
> *planners, developers and shopkeepers, but it*
> *is doubtful if local residents, especially*
> *the elderly, who find it difficult to get about,*
> *are satisfied".*[48]

Fortunately for the inner areas, the shopkeeping
sector has been extensively revitalised by "the new
capitalists", as Peter Hall calls them: the Pakistanis,
Armenians, Ugandan Asians and Chinese. Their entry has
been fortunate, for it offers the prospect of maintaining
the curious role of what used to be called 'ma and pa'
stores in a community where purchasing power is always
low and often erratic. Such shops are more relaxed
about credit than the supermarket, and still offer the
coal in 28 pound bags, the clothing and Christmas clubs,
alongside the newer additions of *"red and green peppers,*
yams, sweet potatoes, okra, aubergines, huaras and
courgettes".[49] Such shops provide for the rhythms of
the community, from a newspaper at 6.0 a.m. through

to a bag of atta flour at 9.30 at night. For this,
however, the community pays the going rate. Not for
them the bulk-buys or freezer-offers: rather the
maximum recommended retail price.

Environment

   To conclude this chapter it may be relevant to
add one or two remarks concerning the inner city
environment. Clearly this involves a series of
general issues, but these can be resolved into the
specific problem of how land is used for different
purposes.

   The most outstanding factor in relation to land-use
is in fact dis-use. Recent studies suggest that
enormous areas within the inner city are simply disused:
in inner London, approximately 2000 acres: 3 square
miles, or about half of one per cent of the entire
Greater London area. In Wigan, the figure rises to a
staggering 12 per cent.[50] One of the points made
consistently within the Inner Area Studies is the futility
of this wastage, at a series of levels. While land
lies idle, it represents a vivid tribute to the decay
of the community and virtually encourages further neglect.
As an environment for children, it can be condemned as
dangerous and unsuitable.

   The problems of pressures upon space manifest
themselves in other ways: there may not be many cars
in the inner cities of Newcastle, but in places like
Oxford the demands of residents, workers, and visitors
produce a scene of congestion, and yet further limitation
upon play space. Except for the occasional adventure
playground, children are forced back upon their own
resources in no-man's land. As the Lambeth study clearly
shows, the environmental impacts of planning (in the
widest sense of the latter term) have too often been
overlooked. Flats are designed with excesses of open

space: communal land to be cared for by all but the responsibility of no-one, and another territory for petty vandalism. One thing worse than cleared land is the redevelopment scheme that leaves isolated homes standing amidst rubble, an immediate target for half a brick, or worse.

These general incompatabilities of the state of the environment, and the needs of residents emerge consistently within the three DOE research reports, and have also been the subject of a follow-up study of would-be movers in Lambeth. Interestingly, to those involved housing and job opportunities are of far less importance than these environmental issues. Whilst 40% of those interviewed wanted to move away from Lambeth in order to improve their surroundings, only 24% gave housing conditions as their main reason and only one percent mentioned employment issues of any description.[51] Thus although we may *objectively* define a set of problems facing inner city residents, those living within these areas have a far simpler *subjective* evaluation of their situation; moreover, anyone who has lived for any length of time in an old decaying core and can remember the impression left by a succession of wet November mornings is likely to go a long way towards agreeing with their priorities.

NOTES AND REFERENCES:

1. Peter Hall, "The Inner cities dilemma", New Society, 3 ✓ February 1977, p. 22.

2. Inner London is defined as the City, Camden, Hackney, Hammersmith, Islington, Kensington and Chelsea, Lambeth, Southwark, Tower Hamlets, Westminster. The middle ring consists of Brent, Greenwich, Haringey, Lewisham, Newham, Waltham Forest, Wandsworth. (See G. Lomas, "Labour and Life in London", in "London: Urban patterns, problems and policies", Heinemann, 1973, p. 38).

3.   R. Drewett, J.B. Goddard, N. Spence, "Whats happening to British cities?", Town and Country Planning, 1976 46, 1, p. 17.

4.   Figures from "New Towns or Inner Cities?", Radio 4 broadcast, 1977, introduced by Noal Boaden.

5.   J. Husain, "Londoners who left", New Society, 7 July 1977, p. 17.

6.   P. Gripaios, "The Closure of firms in the inner city: the South-East London case, 1970-5", Regional Studies, 1977 11, 1, pp. 1-6.

7.   Ibid, p. 2.

8.   B.M.D. Smith, "Employment in inner city areas: A case study of the position in Small Heath, Birmingham in 1974", Working Paper 34, Centre for Urban and Regional Studies, Birmingham, 1975.

9.   Department of the Environment, "Change or decay", H.M.S.O., 1977, p. 43.

10.   P. Gripaios, "The closure of firms in the inner city", Regional Studies, 1977, 11, 1 p. 4.

11.   B.M.D. Smith, "Employment in inner city areas", Working Paper 34, 1975, pp. 36-7.

12.   V.A. Karn, "Housing Associations in the inner city housing market", Paper presented to National Federation of Housing Associations, Inner City Conference, 15-17 July, 1977.

13.   P.J. Taylor, A.M. Kirby, K.J. Harrop, G. Gudgin, Atlas of Tyne-Wear, Newcastle University, Department of Geography, 1976.

14.   S. Holtermann, "Census indicators of urban deprivation", Working Note 6, Department of the Environment, 1975.

15.   S.S. Duncan, "Cosmetic planning or social improvement?", Area, 6, 4, 1974, p. 259-70.

16.   A.M. Kirby, "Housing Action Areas in Great Britain", 1975-77, Geographical Paper 60, Reading, 1977.

17.   Ibid, p. 24.

18.   S.E. Jeffs and A.M. Kirby, "The implications of recent legislation for the public and private rental sectors", Housing Monthly, 12, 12, 1975.

19.   See for example, P. Lawless, "HAAs: powerful attack or financial fiasco?", The Planner, March 1977, p. 39-42.

20.   Housing Policy Consultative Document, Technical Volume, H.M.S.O., 1977.

21.   B. Adams, "Furnished lettings in stress areas", in London, Urban patterns, problems and policies, op. cit.

22.   M. Boddy, "The structure of mortgage finance; Building Societies and the British social formation", Transactions, Institute of British Geographers, NS 1, 1, 1976, pp. 57-71.

23. Ibid, p. 68.

24. J. Short, "Aspects of residential mobility in Bristol", Paper presented to Institute of British Geographers, University of Hull, January 1978.

25. Department of the Environment, "<u>Inner London</u>", H.M.S.O., 1977, p. 156-61.

26. G.W. Shannon and G.E.A. Dever, "<u>Health-care delivery: spatial perspectives</u>", McGraw-Hill, 1974.

27. Department of the Environment, "<u>Area resource analysis, District D tables, 1973-4</u>", DOE, 1974, p. 6.

28. Ibid, p. 7.

29. Department of the Environment, "<u>Change or decay</u>", H.M.S.O., 1977, p. 18.

30. P. Ambrose, "<u>Access and spatial inequality</u>", Open University, 1977, p. 107.

31. J.E. Bradley, A.M. Kirby and P.J. Taylor, "Distance decay and dental decay", <u>Seminar Paper 31</u>, Department of Geography, University of Newcastle-upon-Tyne.

32. D.G. Price and A.J. Cummings, "Family planning clinics in London", <u>Working Paper 2</u>, Polytechnic of Central London.

33. Ibid, p. 14.

34. R.E. Pahl, "Poverty and the urban system", reprinted in <u>Cities, communities and the young</u>, J. Raynor and J. Harden, RKP 1973, p. 102.

35. Ibid, p. 102.

36. Extract from Central Advisory Council for Education, H.M.S.O., 1967, p. 50-1, quoted by D. Herbert, "Urban education; problems and policies", in "<u>Social areas in cities</u>", ed. D. Herbert and R. Johnston, Wiley, 1976, Vol. 2, p. 141.

37. E. Brooks, "Development problems in the inner city", <u>Geographical Journal</u> 141, 3, 1975, pp. 355-362.

38. N. Ferguson, P. Davies, R. Evans, P. Williams, "The Plowden Reports recommendations for identifying children in need of extra help" in Raynor and Harden, op. cit. A far more detailed discussion of this issue is offered by the Inner London Education Authority: see D. Herbert, op. cit., pp. 147-9.

39. Ibid, p. 149.

40. Department of the Environment, "<u>Change or decay</u>", H.M.S.O., 1977, p. 158.

41. R. King, "Social class, educational attainment and provision: an LEA study", <u>Policy and Politics</u>, 3, 1, 1974, pp. 17-35.

42. A.M. Kirby, "The role of the housing market in the process of resource consumption", Paper presented to Institute of British Geographers, University of Hull, January 1978.

43. CDP, "Gilding the ghetto", CDP, 1977.

44. P.J. Taylor, A.M. Kirby, K.J. Harrop, G. Gudgin, "Atlas of Tyne-Wear", Newcastle, 1976, p. 19.

45. Department of the Environment, "Change or decay", H.M.S.O., 1977.

46. A.M. Kirby, K.J. Harrop, "Some preliminary observations concerning the problems of quantitative explanation and social geographic research", North-East Area Study, Working Paper 29, 1976.

47. Department of the Environment, "Change or decay", H.M.S.O., 1977, p. 106.

48. P. Ambrose and B. Colenutt, "The property machine", Penguin Books, 1975, p. 96.

49. Department of the Environment, "Change or decay", H.M.S.O., 1977, p. 50.

50. Civic Trust, "Urban Wasteland", 1977.

51. Department of the Environment, "Study of Intending Migrants", DOE, 1978, p. 22.

Chapter Four

D E P R I V A T I O N

INTRODUCTION

Whilst the preceding chapters have concentrated
upon a general outline of some of the processes at work
within the inner areas and the urban system as a whole,
this is clearly only half the story. Of importance are
the ways in which factors like educational attainment,
job skills and the housing system are all interrelated,
and working to perpetuate and worsen individual problems.
Consequently this chapter attempts to build up a pattern
of the impacts of the phenomena like poor medical services
upon inner city residents. We begin with a general
outline of deprivation.

The Cycle of Deprivation

I have made it clear in the last chapter that there
exists an involved mixture of problems in the inner city,
ranging from shrinking job opportunities through to an
unpleasant general environment. However, it cannot be
assumed that all problems are physical problems, or more
subtly, that all social problems can be solved by
physical planning.[1] There are clearly two strands here:
on the one hand the structural faults that, say, produce
unemployment, and on the other hand the personal factors
that condemn individuals to stress: the loss of a
marriage partner when children are young, or a history
of recurrent mental illness, both problems that make
obtaining, and then holding onto a good job, very
difficult.

The balance that exists between the two sides of
the coin is a difficult one to determine. A recent
study has thoughtfully come to grips with this issue,

examining the role of external forces (like economic recessions) alongside the attitudes of parents in the process of shaping the next generation.[2] As Berthoud points out, a geneticist is likely to opt for a deterministic biological explanation of poverty cycles, i.e., the recurrence of poverty within particular families from generation to generation. The sociologist or economist is more likely to overlook the personal in favour of the social or structural argument. Not surprisingly, both abstract stances have become articles of faith in some quarters: *"the first hypothesis sometimes seems to be used to imply that deprivation is caused by the personal problems of those who get into it; while the second is used to imply that personal problems are a consequence of a society that imposes deprivation on some of its members."* To caricature the two parties concerned, we might call the first a Sir Keith Joseph viewpoint, and the second a Community Development Project outlook.[3]

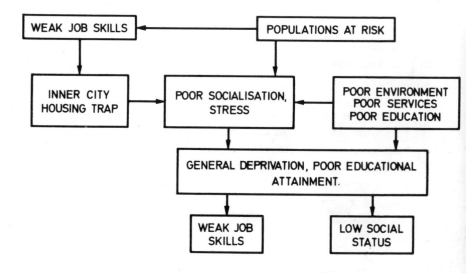

Figure One: A cycle of deprivation within the inner city. See text for details.

I would echo the following statement, which attempts to strike a balance between these views:

> *"(an) apparent focus on the family is too narrow. In the first place, continuities over time regarding high rates of various forms of disadvantage can be seen in terms of schools, inner city areas, social classes, ethnic groups and other social and cultural situations which lie outside the family. Even with respect to familial continuities, the reason for the intergenerational continuity may not be familial at all, but rather may reflect the influence of a common social environment or a common political structure on successive generations."* [4]

In an attempt to outline the processes acting upon the individual, Figure One suggests a simple cycle of deprivation for the inner city. It will be noted that the diagram begins with a population at risk: in this case, blacks, the unskilled, the elderly, as we have suggested. [5] These individuals collectively possess few job skills, and have little purchasing power. They thus find themselves frequently within the inner areas, as a result of the housing trap. Within the core areas, they experience a poor environment; this may produce. or exacerbate, personal stress and as it has been called, a lack of socialisation within children. Put simply, this suggests that development is slowed: as we shall see, for example reading ages may be delayed. In the long term, these effects are manifest as a general level of poor educational attainment amongst children, and an overall atmosphere of hardship, deprivation and disadvantage. In turn, this is likely to result in poor standing within the job market, leading to a new stage within the cycle, and what has been termed low social status. By this is meant that the inner city is frequently socially fragmented, unable to represent its

wishes within the political or planning process, (a point
to be developed at length within the current and subsequent
chapter).

   Clearly, we could begin this discussion at any
stage within the cycle. Let us however concentrate
upon education, an exceptionally contentious issue.

Education and Attainment

   In Chapter Three I suggested that the inner cities
are characterised by both large concentrations of
children from stress backgrounds, and by schools that
are frequently obsolete and in poor repair. As we
shall see, there is no question that children from such
areas do poorly at school: there is a great deal of
debate however as to the importance of the school's
role in this process, and the extent to which further
expenditure can improve performance.

   Let us begin with the question of attainment. This
can be approached in three ways: in terms of *internal*
criteria (for example the pupil being able to move from
one class to the next by showing suitable progress in
reading or writing); in terms of *external* criteria
(emerging at the end of the education process with some
certificates that allow the individual to get a certain
standard of job); or in terms of personal *satisfaction* -
most simply, has the pupil enjoyed school, learnt to
write, read, draw, repair cars, or has he or she been
unhappy, frustrated and absent?

   If we begin with what I have called the internal
measures of attainment, we can find a great deal of
information within the Inner London Education Authority's
Literacy Survey. This covered all eight-year old
children within the ILEA in 1969. At the widest scale,
it was found that the whole range of children had a
reading age approximately six months behind their
chronological age, in comparison with a national sample.

Although comparisons with Outer London boroughs were not available, it was noted within the ILEA that clear distinctions could be made between schools with high scores on an EPA index, and schools with low scores. In the latter, children from all social groups studying within schools of different proportions of these groups (or different 'social mixes'), came close to their expected reading score. Children from higher social groups exceeded their chronological age, whilst children from unskilled manual homes were up to a year behind on average. However, when we look at schools with high EPA scores, we find a very different story. Here, even the few children from high status homes do poorly in comparison, whilst the unskilled manual group is approximately eighteen months behind the anticipated reading level. Not surprisingly, a high "immigrant concentration" within schools also depresses the reading attainment of both black and white children.[6]

A similar picture emerges in the resource analysis carried out within District D in Liverpool, with respect to a test known as the Verbal Reasoning Quotient; this VRQ was used until 1973 as an '11 plus' test. The test is designed so that 25% of pupils should score below 90. In Liverpool as a whole, 37 per cent of pupils scored below 90: however virtually 50 per cent, twice the predicted number, of District D children were below this level.

We would expect that such poor performances would be reflected in similarly weak attainment towards the end of the schooling process. Turning to District D within Liverpool once more, we find that although approximately 8.9% of the city's children of school age live within D, only about 5% of the city's CSE passes are attributed to this area.[7] In Newcastle, similar figures were noted; when we examine A-level results, we find that a pupil attending the comprehensive which draws

heavily on the inner city has only a 1:26 chance of
leaving school with an A-level of any grade. In some
other schools, the probabilities of attaining an A-level
pass are higher than 90%, although it is perhaps worthy
of mention that the results in some local authority
catchment schools are little different from the inner
city scores.[8] I have argued elsewhere that the latter
measure of attainment is of greatest importance for the
individual child, for it is the possession of particular
certificates that increasingly allows access to some
jobs, and restricts entry to others.[9] However, we
should not overlook the qualitative aspects of education:
the extent to which the child enjoys his education. Here
again, we look to measures of failure, unfortunately. As
one observer puts it: *"school, like work after it, is
not so much good or bad; it feels irrelevant. And as
soon as the law allows, you get out"*.[10]

Let us move then from this picture of poor attainment
and performance back to the question of the importance of
the school. If we turn back to the outline of the cycle
of deprivation, we can see that education plays an
important role in the argument. This however has been
comprehensively attacked by Richard Berthoud. Certainly,
he says, it is plausible that poor schools are damaging:
*"if bad schools or bad teachers do not provide bad
education, what is the point of wasting money on good
schools and good teachers?"* These assumptions are
however based upon *"two hypotheses, which, though
obviously reasonable, resolutely refuse to be proved by
any statistical analysis"*.[12]

The first hypothesis is that most deprived children
live in areas of deprivation, which is ultimately the
thinking behind the EPA argument. Berthoud however
draws upon an analysis carried out within the ILEA which
argues that *"the majority of disadvantaged children
are not in disadvantaged areas, and the majority of*

children in disadvantaged areas are not disadvantaged".[13]
The thrust of this finding is that although the at-risk
children and the worst schools were not concentrated
geographically, all the disadvantaged children did
equally badly in terms of attainment. From this Berthoud
concludes that the EPA strategy (concentrating upon *areas*
of deprivation) overlooks a majority of the deprived
pupils, whilst of course if poor attainment is not related
to poor schools, then other factors must be responsible.
These 'other factors' are related by Berthoud to parental
attitudes, which are claimed to account for between 19
and 35 per cent of variations in performance (compared
with between zero and eleven per cent variation in
performance which can be related to school differences).

Let us begin with the suggestion that inner areas
do not have the major concentrations of deprived and
disadvantaged children. This is clearly a statistical,
rather than a commonsense conclusion, which results from
examining nothing but one very large inner area. As
Herbert rightly points out, the suggestion that *"most
poor families do not live in poor areas"* makes little
sense in a perspective of the wider urban system, and
comes from an attempt to compare the bad with the very
bad in terms of deprivation.[14]

The second point deserves greater attention. Just
how important is the school? Clearly, no-one would
suggest that it is all-powerful in shaping the child's
performance. An extremely objective and lucid discussion
on the question of transmitted deprivation has reached
the conclusion that:

> *"substantial intergenerational continuities exist.*
> *It has been well established that genetic factors*
> *play a considerable role in the determination of*
> *individual variations in intelligence. They are of*
> *much less importance with respect to scholastic*
> *attainment, although here too they play some part...*

> *experiential and non-genetic biological influences also have a large effect in raising or lowering intellectual performance. The effect of environmental influences is evident within the normal range...home influences are most important in this respect, but school variables also exert an appreciable effect."*[15]

The latter comment rather contradicts Berthoud's stance that *"observed differences in performance are almost entirely explained in terms of differences in the quality of the (school) intake",*[16] although this statement can be related to particular empirical examples. It will be remembered for example that one study related the proportions of working-class children to attainment within a school, and found quite high relationships - the greater the proportions, the lower the aggregate performance, despite far higher expenditure and better staff provision.[17]

The problem with this sort of analysis is that it does not compare like with like. All studies regard it as unlikely that *"the slightly higher level of expenditure in EPA schools on staffing and materials alone can compensate for the extra amounts that richer families spend on books or games equipment for their children, let alone for the disadvantages of poverty and over-crowding".*[18] In order to get to grips with this problem of understanding, one must compare inner city school with inner city school, in order to evaluate on the one hand the impacts of expenditure, and on the other the required levels of spending for future strategies. As yet, these topics have not been tackled. The only research that has realistically compared like with like is an analysis by sociologists at LEA scale, where it appears that attainment *is* a reflection of the levels of expenditure by the Local Education Authority.[19] As for the amounts of expenditure that would be required in order

to offer true equality of opportunity, these would
clearly be enormous. Examples from the medical literature
suggest that the disadvantages imposed by environment and
home require highly intensive attention before they can
be overcome.[20] In part, however, this topic involves
some recognition of "social education" at the expense
of "formal education", as we saw in Chapter Three.
Whilst it can be argued that *"current education is an
almost exclusively upper-middle social class concern
providing that group with certificates"*, and that *"such
a service is of little or no value to the children of
the lowest social class even if it was provided in
sufficient quantity and quality in the inner areas"*,
there remains the question of alternatives.[21] Simmie
has expressed this issue concisely, and I quote him at
length:

> *"Part of the dilemma is to decide whether the
> children should be trained to fill the low-skilled
> jobs which may be available to them, or whether they
> should be educated to expect something which most
> of them, under present conditions, may not attain.
> If they are trained for the former, they are likely
> to perpetuate rather than break the poverty cycle.
> If they are educated to expect the latter, then a
> potential for anomie and conflict is generated.
> Frequently in deprived areas these already take
> the form of delinquency and crime".*[22]

It would be possible to merge this section into a
consideration of poor socialisation, manifest as
delinquency. However, I intend to concentrate initially
on the central themes within the cycle of deprivation,
and to link education with job opportunities.

Poverty and Low Incomes

In any study of employment, it is dangerous to make
generalisations about qualifications and incomes: for

example some unskilled workers earn more than skilled
non-manual salaried staff, on account of overtime
opportunities, payments for risk and so on. Equally, a
third of manual workers possess formal academic
qualifications, (in the engineering trades for example)
whilst a third of non-manual workers, on the other hand,
lack any formal training (in the clerical services, for
instance). When we come to apply these principles to
families in the inner city, they do however assume
clearer definition, simply because the labour market is
so constrained. As we saw in Chapter Three, job
opportunities in the inner areas are severely curtailed,
and continue to contract. For the man without a
marketable skill, or the recent school-leaver lacking a
clutch of O- and A-levels, openings can be very hard to
find: *"the general direction of change is away from
heavy industry, and jobs done by male manual workers,
towards light industry and office qualifications, and
the routine tasks are mainly performed by women"*.[23]

The process is outlined in greater detail by the CDP:
*"warehousing and distribution are the real growth
industries of these areas today. Most of the
demand for vacant industrial premises is for these
sorts of uses. Increasingly these areas are becoming
places to store goods made elsewhere. Everything
is stored there - from new and costly products like
pharmaceuticals at one end of the scale to used
cars and scrap at the other.*

*What about the new jobs brought in to the areas
by these sorts of activities? Most of these offer
low wage rates and involve little skill. Over
two-thirds of those who worked as warehousemen in
1974 earned less than £40 per week, compared to
one-third of semi-skilled workers in traditional
industries"*.[24]

The Community Development Project outlines a series

of stark choices: basically to accept unemployment,
or to become poorly-paid. In Canning Town, redundancies
at Tate and Lyle's led to many workers increasing the
lengths, and costs of their journeys to work, whilst
actually lowering their take-home pay in jobs like
caretaking, hospital portering, post sorting or security
guarding. Given the degree of public-spending cuts in
the last two years, even the poorest jobs in the public
sector have only marginal security.

Alongside this slide from skilled work to low pay
are those who do not recover from redundancy. If jobs
are not quickly replaced, confidence disappears, and
the individual's job history begins to look more and more
unattractive. *"The loss of a job diminishes confidence.
This reduces effective social contacts outside the home
and focusses tension within the family. In turn this
reduces the support the family can give and so reduces
confidence still further"*.[25] At the bottom of the heap
are those who have never had a job: a recent study
suggests that nearly two-thirds of the 16-18 year olds
without qualifications were unemployed for greater than
six months: less than half of those with CSE qualifications
were out of work for such a length of time.[26]

These problems are national, if not indeed
international. However, as we would now expect, the
inner city magnifies and intensifies causes, impacts and
results: *"a major part of the explanation for the
youth unemployment problem in Lambeth lies in the sizeable
proportion of West Indians in the younger age groups of
the workforce. Black youths suffer from a combination
of disadvantages in the job market, including problems
with language, literacy and education, problems with
families and homelessness, unrealistic expectations and,
of course, racial discrimination. Initial failure
resulting from these and from lack of local manual jobs
would naturally reinforce tendencies to a sense of*

alienation, job instability, and resort to crime."[27]

To summarise this discussion, inner city workers are disadvantaged in two ways. The *nature* of the disadvantage is really no different from that faced by poorly-skilled workers in any location: the life expectancy is always lower, the occupational mortality rates higher, the likelihood of receiving a second pension lower, for example. However the degree of deprivation is concentrated. The first strand of the argument relates, as we have seen to unemployment. Berthoud suggests that living at or around the Supplementary Benefit or National Insurance level *"is just about enough to live adequately on, if members of the households include both a <u>first-class housekeeper and a first-class domestic lawyer</u>".*[28] (original emphasis) Budgeting is important, because of the proportions of the income taken up by food, transport, and heating: exactly the areas that have shown consistent inflation since 1974. Although it is a common sentiment (one of many unsubstantiable assertions) that those living 'on welfare' are work-shy, affluent and all have colour televisions (obtained naturally from the Social Services Department), it seems on balance that the majority of those living on low-incomes are in hardship, and solely as a result of the shortage of income, not the size of the outgoings. In part this is a function of the complexity of the whole benefits spectrum: from actually finding out *where* to apply through to knowing about what is available, is a jungle of lost opportunities such as one million unclaimed rate rebates in 1974.

On the other side of the coin, it is a mistake to overemphasise the relationship between unemployment and poverty, as this overlooks the large number of households living on small wage-packets. As we have seen, low pay is a function of the job, but is artificially maintained through the pressures to stay in work, which cause

employees to overlook poor overtime opportunities and
weak trade union representation. Low incomes hit
especially hard families with young children, both because
of the higher outgoings, but also as a result of the
problems facing the working woman with a family. (In
parenthesis, it may be noted that studies have attempted
to relate the high rate of child-minding experienced by
West Indian children to poor intellectual and language
development). Of particular importance for families
in this situation is the *poverty trap*, whereby a small
increase in earnings (say from overtime or upgrading)
simply results in a loss of benefits because a particular
threshold for allowances has been passed. Furthermore,
constant changes in benefit levels can lead to a situation
whereby to claim for one source of aid (e.g. rent and
rate rebates) could lead to a loss of another, such as
free school meals, actually worth more than the first
benefit. *"A three-child family on £69 a week gross has
(if we assume that £10 is their weekly rent and rates)
net disposable resources of £53.01, while a similar
family earning £76 a week gross ends up only 13p a week
better off."*[29]

So far we have not explicitly linked up the employment
chances of those leaving school at present with varying
levels of educational attainment beyond the suggestion
that unemployment in inversely related to qualifications.
This however is only half the story. Again, to concentrate
upon unemployment statistics hides the nature of the jobs
being taken by youngsters (whilst also distracting
attention away from the most serious cases of unemployment,
notably the middle-aged male with dependent children).[30]
An escape from the inner areas is most likely to be
achieved via the social mobility gained through a good
job: and yet the employment statistics are not
reassuring. In Liverpool, boys and girls getting
unskilled work exceed the proportions of both the North-East

and Britain as a whole: two-thirds of school-leavers in
1972 for example. In 1974, only 38 per cent of boys,
and 16 per cent of girls were receiving any formal
industrial training, compared with figures for the
North-West as a whole of 55 and 28 per cent respectively.
And as the Lambeth study observes, *"if someone failed
to start on apprenticeship or traineeship on leaving
school, second chances were difficult to find."*[31]

If social mobility is constrained, then geographical
mobility may appear the answer. The next section
investigates the impacts of the housing market upon
those wanting to move away from the inner areas.

Housing and Mobility

It is no exaggeration to suggest that the housing
market is a major obstacle to geographical mobility. At
the national scale, there is little doubt that more
poorly-skilled workers would have moved to the work, if
such a thing were easily accomplished. However, the
gradient of house prices for the mover from a region of
unemployment to one of employment opportunities operates
against the mover, whilst the possibilities of a
council house exchange or transfer over such a distance
are remote. The usual alternative is for the male worker
to move alone, living in rented accommodation and
attempting to bring the family at a later date. Not
surprisingly, inertia tends to gain the upper hand in
the face of such choices.

For the inner city resident, this process operates
even if the prospective move is only within the same
town or city. As I have suggested, privately-rented
accommodation is hard to find outside the inner areas,
simply because the economics of landlordism offer such
poor returns. A large-scale enterprise would need to
concentrate upon the luxury market, whilst the small-
scale landlord, perhaps inheriting a suburban semi-,

would be well-advised to sell rather than to rent.

In relation to owner-occupied housing, the story is the same. As far as house prices are concerned, the inner area represents in the main the point of lowest costs within the city. Before the potential migrant can buy something more expensive, he needs financial assistance, and before he can obtain a mortgage, he needs to show a stable job prospect. Importantly, a large income is less useful than a guaranteed one that does not depend upon overtime or bonuses to be achieved. In the main, it is unlikely that those trying to leave the core areas will possess this sort of job.

The third main sector, that of council housing, does offer in theory some prospect of mobility. In practice however this is not easily achieved. Let us take the case first of all of the long-distance migrant who has perhaps moved from the North-East or Ireland, or further afield: say the Indian sub-continent. As we have seen, it is likely that the mover will be a lone male, although he may of course bring his family with him, or send for them soon after arrival. Upon arrival he may try for local authority accommodation, only to find that he must fulfil some sort of residence qualification. This varies from District to District: in the past, London Boroughs operated a minimum requirement of five years within Greater London, plus perhaps also a year within the Borough receiving the application. Whilst this may seem a superficially fair way of allocating scarce resources to those who have been in some nominal queue for the longest time, it does tend to have serious overtones and implications. In the past, local authorities have blatantly attempted to give low preference to "immigrants" (Blacks, Irish), *"as for instance in the case of the London Metropolitan Borough which told the Milner Holland Committee that it gave more points for being native British than living in damp insanitary conditions.*"[32]

    The results of this type of policy have been closely documented by John Rex, the sociologist, in a study of Sparkbrook, Birmingham. He noted that Asian immigrants were constrained to live in inner city rented accommodation whilst they came to terms with the requirements of the housing market, and that during this period of assimilation they were often in some stress. From this analysis, Rex went on to identify "housing classes". Rather than emphasising *social* classes, which are determined by the economic order and the individual's place within it, he concentrated upon accessibility to, and possession, of housing. Whilst recognising that the former affects the individual's place in the housing queue, *"it is also the case that amongst those who share the same relation to the means of production there may be considerable differences in ease of access to housing."*[33] The housing classes are outlined in Table 9:

TABLE NINE: THE THEORY OF HOUSING CLASSES, AFTER REX

Housing Class	Likely Location
Owners of Large Houses	Suburbs, Rural Areas
Mortgage Payers in Desirable Houses	Suburbs
Council Tenants in Council Built Homes	Outer Estates, New Towns
Council Tenants in CPO Property Awaiting Demolition	Inner Areas
Tenants of Private Home Owners	"Inner Ring"
House Owners with Lodgers	Inner Areas
Lodgers in Rooms	Inner Areas

The migrant, and especially the black immigrant, is likely to begin at the very bottom of the pile, as a

lodger in rooms, before moving on to become a private
tenant. This partial move up the housing class ladder
tends then to be followed by a respite, whilst the
chance to springboard into another sector of housing
is sought. As we have seen, Asian families are keen
to purchase property: in fact Rex's analysis is rather
undermined by the fact that his study of immigrants
overlooks that they are not in the main conscious of
local authority residence qualifications, because they
rarely apply for council housing. Indeed, a study in
Newcastle-upon-Tyne showed that some Asian families
had reached the coveted stage of being within clearance
property. When the Housing Department made an offer
of a property, it was refused: the family would then
move to and buy another house within the vicinity.
This had happened to some families two, or even
three times.[34]

This does not, I think, undermine Rex's general
argument, especially with regard to the problems facing
those trying to cross over into local authority housing.
As the recent Housing Green Paper has again argued,
tenants in private accommodation are rarely able to
plan for the future, simply because they do not know
how they stand in the waiting list. Different
priorities are given by different Authorities to
different sets of circumstances: in some Districts,
for example, teachers can still leap-frog the queue
at the expense of large families with poor accommodation.

More worrying is the allocation process operated
by Housing Departments with respect to first time
tenants. There is a good deal of evidence that, again,
housing need is subordinated to some assessment of the
potential stability of the family in question. This
seems not unreasonable: the Housing Department is
responsible for efficient and cheap management of
property, as well as the overcoming of housing need.

However, it is clear that the family in stress conditions may be hard put to demonstrate that they are "good tenants". A recent study in Hull has shown that the fairly junior officials responsible for visiting those on the waiting list have very narrow pre-conceptions: being coloured and possessing long-hair are immediate grounds for suspicion it seems.[35] The opposite also seems to be true; in Newcastle-upon-Tyne, and Derby, elite council estates have been noted. Typically, they are close to owner-occupied parts of the city, have proportionately high rateable values, and are occupied by a very different cross-section of households than those found generally within council housing. The numbers of households from the unskilled categories are very low, for example: a curious finding given that local authority housing is usually associated with the lower-income household in housing need.[36]

These findings are usually subsumed under the heading of "managerialist": that is, an investigation of the actors involved in this sort of situation, in an attempt to understand a little better the decision-making process. The ideas of managerialism have been summarised by Ray Pahl as follows: *"the planners, social workers, housing managers and so forth are very often trying to turn the taps of their resources to favour the most disadvantaged; but either through a mistaken belief in the validity of their data, a lack of awareness of unintended consequences of their actions, or simply through human error, the results of their activity fail to improve, or possibly add to the plight of the poor".*[37]

In the case of the household trying to enter the local authority sector, any suspicion of being a "problem family" is likely to result in the offer of a property being restricted to either a further non-purpose built property, or increasingly in some cities,

a decayed block of flats, such as the recently-
demolished Quarry Hill block in Leeds, Noble Street
in Newcastle, Ferguslie Park in Paisley - all
essentially inner-city areas.[38]

> *"A number of smaller estates and tower blocks*
> *have become notorious with a high vacancy rate,*
> *and for council estates, a comparatively high*
> *rate of turnover of population. They contain*
> *greater proportions of single parent families,*
> *new commonwealth immigrants, or problem*
> *families, chiefly as a result of rehousing*
> *families from nearby clearance areas, or taking*
> *in those who had little choice of where to live."*[39]

It will be remembered that this section began with
a general aim of discussing mobility, and yet all
avenues appear to lead consistently back to the inner
areas. Of course, once in the local authority sector,
it is quite possible to apply for transfer or exchange.
The latter is unlikely to evoke much response, and it
has been found that for most households, the possibilities
of achieving a successful transfer tend to be poor.
A joint study of London and Newcastle-upon-Tyne showed
that successful transfer cases had waited between two
and four and a half years for that transfer.[40] Different
types of families were more likely to be successful than
others in obtaining a move: for example, families
living in over-crowded conditions frequently found it
difficult to get the Housing Department to agree that
they needed more space. Couples or single persons
with homes now too big for their needs were however
more likely to be moved, as were the elderly, with a
large 'points score' based on illness or infirmity.
The destination of the move also determines the chance
of the transfer being quickly obtained: naturally
enough, a move within the inner area will be
accomplished with less difficulty than a move to one

of the elite estates mentioned above. As the Liverpool Inner Area Study however points out, the 1974 Local Government reorganisation meant that some Metropolitan Districts were separated from parts of their hinterlands - Liverpool itself can no longer draw upon the Cantrill Farm area of high-quality council dwellings, for example.

To summarise this section then, it becomes easier to see just why the inner areas still possess large numbers of inhabitants who are unable to move away into either homes bought, or homes to rent. The Stockwell Study found that approximately half the households in the area wanted to leave, but concludes that *"they are trapped by the workings of the housing market rather than the labour market".* [41]

Personal Stress

Whilst the strands that link up qualifications, job opportunities and housing chances are primarily determined by the existence of fairly concrete phenomena like council housing policies, there is also a second area of deprivation within the cycle of disadvantage that relates far more to individual problems. Questions of personal stress have received a great deal more attention in the past, especially from American sociologists who have coined patronising terms for parts of the inner city, such as 'Hobohemia'. The emphasis is upon the role that the inner areas have to play within the social system: they represent a physical expression of deviance, of being different in some way:

> *"normally, in every city, there is a fashionable area: and another area occupied by artists, intellectuals and actors, who may not have very high incomes, but are prepared to live a bohemian life and do not demand very high standards of housing."* [42]

This sort of thinking has even been placed in formal
terms: *"of the inner city population...the cosmopolites
include students, artists, writers, musicians and
entertainers...(who) rear children in the city especially
if they have the income to afford the aid of servants
and governesses. The less affluent ones may move to
the suburbs, continuing to live as cosmopolites under
considerable handicaps."*[43] Rather than examine the
more obvious proposition that students, artists et al
are generally not affluent (few students possess
governesses in my experience), and thus live in the
inner areas for the same reasons as everyone else,
Gans suggests that *"they live in the city in order to
be near the special 'cultural' facilities that can
only be located near the center (sic) of the city."*[44]

Although examples like the one above are extreme,
it is frequently assumed that inner areas can perform
a service, of sorts, by providing anonymity to, say,
homosexuals, prostitutes, and as we shall see, those
prone to breakdown. As a half-way house explanation,
this is superficially logical - that social deviance
should be mirrored by special places for deviance to
go on. It is almost a liberal attitude, until one
thinks it through. In the first place it assumes that
deviants are in need of refuge - perhaps they would
prefer not to be thought of as deviant in the first
place. Secondly, as already suggested, it ignores
the fact that those with, for example, personality
problems are likely to be economically weak, with all
that this entails.

Whilst bearing these questions in mind, let us
look more systematically at what David Herbert has
called 'social deviance' in his excellent review of
the subject.

We can begin with what is sometimes called medical
geography: in other words the distributions of disease.

Clearly, there are three factors at work here that are
relevant to an examination of the inner city environment.
Firstly, there is the incidence of disease that results
from some source within the inner areas. Secondly, there
is the incidence that reflects neglect, or poor access
to treatment. Thirdly, there is the question, already
mentioned, of individuals already suffering from
illness moving into the core areas.

In respect to the first category, the most famous
example is that of the cholera epidemics that were
eventually traced back to contaminated wells in parts
of London in the last century. Equally dramatic
examples are not to be found in contemporary cities,
nor are medical statistics generally available for
parts of cities. It does seem likely however that
rates of pollution in many inner areas have until
recently been consistently higher, due to the central
location of many industrial enterprises, and that
attendant respiratory complaints will have been higher
too. A recent study of London, for example, notes that:

> *"the third component, air-pollution, living
> conditions and respiratory diseases, offers much
> more scope for interpretation. Like the first
> it includes both measures of air pollution, but
> in this case it singles out those boroughs in
> which higher-than-average concentrations of smoke
> and sulphur di-oxide in the air occur in
> conjunction with respiratory diseases, bad housing
> conditions and mortality at birth. It therefore
> brings together a group of variables in an almost
> classic syndrome typifying the unhealthy urban
> environment."*[46]

Whilst some of the Boroughs that score badly on this
measure are suburban ones like Waltham Forest that
are suffering from the prevailing wind, the preponderance
of ill-health is within the central area - Lambeth,

Southwark, Tower Hamlets, Islington, for example.

Moving on to the second category, that of illness through neglect or lack of facilities, we are again limited by a shortage of statistics. In the USA, several studies have shown a high incidence of physical disease, such as *"heart disease, tuberculosis, diabetes, syphilis, cirrhosis of the liver, amoebic dysentery, bacillary dysentery and salmonellosis"* within inner areas.[47] As far as the Inner Area Studies are concerned, we know for example that in Small Heath and Stockwell, 21 per cent and 29 per cent of families respectively were typified by some sort of disability, and of course over half the retired households living in poverty were suffering from health problems.[48] The extent to which these figures reflect health problems stemming from the environment (exacerbated perhaps by bad housing), poor health-care facilities, from poverty in general (badly balanced diet for example) or occupational injury, can only be guessed at however.

I have already introduced in Chapter Three the study of schizophrenia in Nottingham, which found that almost 70 per cent of cases admitted to hospitals between 1963 and 1969 were living within four kilometres of the city centre. Whilst the author attributed this finding to environmental stress, I have also introduced the far more rational explanation which connects the incidence of mental illness to location via the housing market. As with the case of education, clearly there are a number of factors to disentangle here. For example, rates of psychiatric disorder have been found to be higher too for children: a study comparing incidence within Inner London and the Isle of Wight found that general disorders were *"truly twice as common in inner London"*[49] for both adults and children. This might seem to rule out the housing factor: the study, on closer investigation however noted that *"city life*

had little <u>direct</u> adverse effect on children, but
rather that the effects were mediated through the
family".[50] Stress resulting from poor housing, a
lack of social cohesion, loneliness, were all considered
but found to be unimportant.

Are further pointers to be found in the literature
on mental disturbance? One statistic is that 99 per
cent of Nottingham's foreign-born patients lived within
the inner city; but there again, so do a very large
proportion of immigrant groups, as we have seen. One
other finding, that could be thought to contradict the
housing market thesis, was noted in London where
similar rates were recorded for both those moving into
the area, and those born and bred within the core.
Without conjecturing too deeply about cycles of
intergenerational disturbance, we must probably accept
Rutter and Madge's conclusions that

"the reasons why disorder remains at a relatively
high rate among inner city dwellers are likely
to be rather different from the reasons why
psychiatric problems are found in succeeding
generations of the Smith family but not among
the Browns".[51]

Questions of disorder merge imperceptibly into the
case of suicide, which is partly a medical phenomenon
on one hand, and a deviant act on the other. Although
less research has been done on suicide, some studies
"have frequently linked high suicide rates to lodging
house areas with their transient, lone occupants".[52]
Again the question of cause and effect (i.e. does the
housing market bring those with a prediliction for
suicide to the inner city, or does the environment
carry some residents over the edge) remains unanswered.

In turn, suicide, until recently a criminal act,
segues into an examination of crime and delinquency.

One of the recurring themes within the Inner Area

Studies is that of the disruption caused to neighbourhoods
by crime, especially petty violence and mugging: within
the household surveys, respondents frequently commented
upon this, and also tended to link crime with racial
groups. As Herbert shows, there is some truth in the
residents' feelings that their areas have high rates
of petty crime (car break-ins for example) vandalism
and mugging: however the extent to which this sort of
non-professional crime is imported from other parts of
the city by individuals or groups using central city
facilities like clubs or football grounds needs to be
determined. Studies in Cardiff show that inner city
areas have quite high concentrations of delinquents in
residence, but that local authority housing estates
out on the fringes of the city have equally high
concentrations.

In studies focussed more fixedly upon the inner
city, a more detailed picture of behaviour patterns
and links with the environment has been built up. The
Liverpool Inner Area Study for example presents the
following history in sympathetic terms:

*"In his study of an inner city tenement estate
in Liverpool, Howard Parker suggested a development
of delinquency which started at about eight years
of age, rose to a peak of organised theft from
sixteen to eighteen and then tailed off with
girlfriends and marriage.*
*The youngest were found to graduate from
acceptable naughtiness to petty pilfering in a
social environment in which the availability of
stolen goods was taken for granted, yet theft
as such was frowned upon. By the time they were
ten or twelve the group had become local hard-men,
and moved easily from theft from cars to joyriding
and shoplifting. By their late teens most had
begun to withdraw into the more normal social*

89

> *structure of the neighbourhood; leading to*
> *fairly regular work, marriage and a nearby*
> *council flat."* [53]

Explanations for this behaviour are mixed. Sociologists
have produced theories of sub-culture that suggest
simply that deviance is a response to a recognition
that 'normal' social goals are not easily achieved.
Other studies, such as Herbert's, emphasise the
attitudes of parents to misbehaviour, and the simple
facts of circumstance - homelessness amongst juveniles
for example is a frequent precursor to theft. Similarly,
large families, small homes and inadequate play space
can all lead to a minimum of supervision in young
children. The physical fabric of the inner areas can
also actively encourage misuse; as we have seen, many
new estates have an excess of neutral space, that is
no-one's responsibility. Property too is left to decay:
the Liverpool study criticises the Local Authority in
this respect, for virtually inviting vandalism against
some dwellings and commercial buildings.

Clearly then, there are examples of high rates
of deviance amongst inner city residents, although the
extent to which the statistics of say, suicide, can
ultimately be related back to the environment on the
one hand, intergenerational traits on the other, plus
the sorting effects of the housing market, remains to
be fully determined. To conclude this section, it
may however be worthwhile to introduce two further
points. The first is the one-sidedness of deviance
statistics used in much of the academic literature.
As both Herbert and Pahl are keen to point out, the
inner city does not figure largely in tax crimes,
which in monetary terms are far more important to the
economy as a whole than crimes against property. [54] In
other words, there may be an overemphasis upon the
more visible and sensational acts of anti-social behaviour.

The second point relates to the longevity of deviance.
The Liverpool study suggests that there exist definite
cycles of behaviour, that normally tail off into
'normal' patterns as adulthood approaches. This is a
point worthy of emphasis with respect to problem
families. A good deal of publicity is given to those
households like the one sketched by the Lambeth team:
the husband regularly unemployed, changing jobs four
times in five years, had recently assaulted a counter
clerk at the Supplementary Benefits Commission Office.
He had a history of violence, and was facing having the
electricity cut off for large arrears, despite the fact
that a new colour television had just been hired. This
story has now become almost a caricature of 'the Rough',
and yet as the Stockwell survey shows, most families
in poverty display very different reactions to their
situation. *"Even on the widest interpretation, no more
than about one in six or seven or those interviewed
could be so described. This suggests that such households amounted to fewer than one in 40 in Stockwell".*[55]
It seems fair to suggest therefore that both extreme
pictures of the inner city, the one emphasising its
positive role, the other the large numbers of problem
families are, as we might expect, misleading.

Community Consciousness

Whilst one path within the cycle of disadvantage
terminates at 'low job skills' (although this is
naturally not the end of the story), it can be seen
that the other line in Figure One comes to rest at
'low social status'. This clearly needs some
explanation.

To the sociologist, social status is, as I have
already briefly outlined, different from but complementary
to, social class. The latter is to do with the economic
scheme of things, whilst social status is a function of

consumption. Housing classes are a measure of social
status, and it is possible to talk of status groups
in terms of education and health: in other words,
high social status can be fashioned by the access to
good housing, in localities where there are good
private schools, community health facilities and so on.
As far as the inner city is concerned, the opposite
tends to be the case in most instances.

Status is of importance because we can link it up
with notions of community, which in turn are connected
to the political process. For a locality to present
its needs and views coherently to a local council, it
needs to have some consensus of views, and some
willingness to access the political machine. One
of the most interesting aspects of latterday social
science is the increasing emphasis upon the ways in
which normal political cleavages (at the very simplest
of levels, party politics) can be transcended by local
(spatial, or community) needs. Obvious examples here
are ways in which places like Cublington, threatened
by the building of the Third London Airport, come
together to resist the plans.[56] For such community
consciousness to exist, it seems that a threat is
necessary: consensus comes out of conflict. However,
status fits in here, for naturally a neighbourhood
must be worth fighting for in the face of some change.
There are in this vein a number of studies that show
how inner city areas are poorly placed to develop a
community sense in the face of changes to the area.
A classic study in Newcastle-upon-Tyne shows the ways
in which bungled plans to redevelop a part of the inner
area could not transcend the differences of interest
within the neighbourhood (owner-occupiers, tenants,
landlords, blacks, whites, old and young): for much
of a decade, the area sank slowly into greater decay,
and was unable to shake off the stigma that was

increasingly associated with its name.[57]

A number of such studies have pointed to some
general factors that must be achieved before community
action can be successful. Firstly, the local political
action, such as tenant co-operatives or squatters'
associations, must attract traditional political
support within the council chamber.[58] This however
is difficult, due to the low interest in traditional
politics on the one hand, (inner city turnout at
local elections is frequently as low as 15 or 20
per cent of the electorate) and the lack of association
with the area on the other; few councillors live in
inner area wards, perhaps for obvious reasons. These
divisions lead to mistrust and ignorance: *"in inner
Liverpool, at any rate, there was an enormous gap
between 'them and us'"*.[59]

However, these gulfs do not exist simply between
the political machine and the residents, but more
importantly between the planners and the planned. The
story learnt from recent inquiries into road - provision
schemes is that communities can only gain even the
most partial successes by debating on technical and/or
legal issues.[60] Again, these require skill,
articulation and professional help. All are normally
available in suburban and rural areas, but not so
readily in inner cities.

In consequence of this gap between city hall and
those at the receiving end of the planning process, the
inner areas of most conurbations are marked by planning
blight - the detritus and decay that come from long-term
strategies only partly achieved. In Liverpool again,
11 per cent of the studied area was derelict land, of
which three-quarters was held by the council for
redevelopment. However, some of the long-term
strategies had come and gone: the 1966 Transportation
Plan has been changed out of recognition, because of

poor forecasts in car-ownership. Shopping precincts
too have remained unbuilt. *"A combination of over-*
ambitious planning, cumbersome and centralised management
and ineffective monitoring has resulted in a depressing
state of physical chaos".[61]

Nor are the cores simply affected by planning blight.
Some inner city zones, especially where they abut
prosperous central business districts, have been at
times very attractive to developers. Bob Colenutt
has recounted the ways in which Southwark council
undertook major redevelopment schemes in the early
1970's in partnership with commercial interests. Only
limited local opposition developed due to the lack of
consultation undertaken by the Borough, and small firms
and houses were cleared, to be replaced by offices,
restaurants and attendant services. Colenutt sees
the development process as removing housing and employment,
and replacing them with facilities of use only to those
living outside the Borough: *"from the subsequent*
invasion of office development and blight, the property
industry has been the clear beneficiary, with the local
community the outright loser."[62]

This is not to suggest that inner areas are totally
devoid of community groups. The Liverpool study
documents community councils, tenants' associations and
more specific groups relating to particular projects
like play. David Donnison shows the way in which a
host of organisations can bring their influence to bear
on seemingly unlikely issues:

> *"Islington Borough Council proposed in 1969*
> *to close a set of public baths...within a few*
> *days the Council was being lobbied by the*
> *Islington Society, the Canonbury Society, the*
> *Barnsbury Association, and local groups and*
> *branches of the Consumers Association, the*
> *Association of State Education, the Fabian*

> *Society, the Swimming Teachers, the primary school*
> *heads, the Sub-Aqua Club, old-age pensioners*
> *(users of hot-baths), orthodox jewry (users of*
> *the bath for men only) and others."*[63]

In the final analysis however community consciousness,
community action, public participation, or even *"urban
social movements"*[64] are only a reaction to a threat:
*"it is difficult to see the growth of community action
in Liverpool as anything other than a response to trends
in local authority activity."*[65] The question of
involving inner areas in the next round of forward
planning will be problematic: *"all of this points to
a key element in public involvement in the decision-
making process: the degree of public awareness
concerning the relevance for the community and the
individual of the issues presented for discussion and
comment. Hence a high degree of involvement in the
urban renewal process, and a very low response to
strategic planning issues".*[66] Furthermore, besides
the question of involvement in the formal planning
process, there is the question of 'self-help', which
as we shall see in Chapter Five is stressed by parts
of the Inner Area Reports as being vital to future
revitalisation. As with participation, it will however
be very difficult for residents to overlook past
mistakes, and to imagine that some watershed in their
fortunes has been reached. Liverpool, for example has
already witnessed every type of area-based improvement
policy from an EPA in 1969 up to and including an Area
Management scheme as part of the Inner Area investigation.
In areas like Lambeth, residents have tried repeatedly
to sort out their own housing problems, even showing
the initiative to form a Housing Association designed
to patch up short-life council property lying empty.
However, even when the community tried to do the local
authority's job for it (a curious reversal of the

democratic process), opposition from elected representatives and officials consistently hamstrung the enterprise.[67] In consequence, any 'New Deal' is going to have to gain local support not simply by exhortation, as in the past, but by example, and results.

Summary

This chapter has tried to get to grips with the most fundamental issue of poverty, namely the relationships between people on the one hand, and the causes of the problems that they face on the other. The National Community Development Project observes, with respect to the inner cities, *"that such areas can be identified by physical overcrowding, high unemployment rates, dereliction and decay is not disputed; the distortion comes as the focus is turned on the people, not the environment or the wider structural causes. The implicit metaphor of illness is ever present: people are 'suffering' from 'chronic' deprivation."*[68] Of course, the residents *are* suffering: but from an illness caused by attrition, not self-neglect. Here, I have argued that it is the wider issues - industrial decline, local authority policy, government housing policies, that operate as the template within which disadvantage must be understood. Stress and an inability to cope, at individual and at group levels, exist, but their importance is marginal, and their cause is again as much a product of the environment as a personal defect.

This conclusion, like that of the CDP, is not in step with local or central government policy. *"The usefulness to the state of defining the urban problem to the residents of the older industrial areas as a sickness to be 'treated' hardly needs stressing. It fits neatly along-side the idea that it is a marginal*

problem to be solved by increased discussion - with
the Neighbourhood Council acting as a surgery, and the
Area Management team as medical consultants."[69]
Essentially, these views mark out the battle lines on
the policy issue, although as we shall see, the range
of ideas on how inner city problems are to be ameliorated
is anything but narrow.

NOTES AND REFERENCES: CHAPTER FOUR

1.   A mature discussion of the implicit assumptions of the
     planning process may be found in T.A. Broadbent, "Planning
     and profit in the urban economy", Methuen, 1977.

2.   R. Berthoud, "The disadvantages of inequality", PEP, 1976.

3.   See for example Chapter One of CDP, "Gilding the ghetto",
     CDP, 1977.

4.   M. Rutter and N. Madge, "Cycles of disadvantage", HEB,
     1977, p. 6.

5.   A constant criticism of many sociological models is that
     they fail to go beyond identification of phenomena and
     thus answer the fundamental problems about why things
     come about. Clearly, to merely identify "populations
     at risk" falls into this category. To suggest that some
     households are weak in the housing market overlooks the
     questions of why the housing market operates in such a
     manner, and why particular households are discriminated
     against: see for example S.S. Duncan, "Research directions
     in social geography", Transactions of the Institute of
     British Geographers, NS 1, 1, 1976, p. 17. Although this
     problem will be returned to within the text, I fundamentally
     accept a veiw of the housing market which suggests that it
     is structured as an adjunct of capital, and that access
     should be seen in ultimately in terms of production (i.e.
     social class determined in the work place) and not solely
     in relation to consumption, (i.e. social status derived
     from the possession of a particular type of property).

6.   A. Little and C. Mabey, "Reading Attainment and Social
     and Ethnic Mix of London Primary Schools", in D. Donnison
     and D. Eversley, "London, urban patterns, problems and
     policies", Heinemann, 1973.

7.   Department of the Environment, "Area resource analysis:
     District D. Tables, 1973-4", DOE, 1974, p. 40.

8.   A.M. Kirby, "A constrained model of residential land-use",
     unpublished Ph.D. thesis, Newcastle, 1978, Chapter Seven.

9.   Ibid, p. 178.

10. B. Jackson, "How the poorest live: education", New Society, February 1, 1973.

11. R. Berthoud, "The disadvantages of inequality", PEP, 1976, p. 115.

12. Ibid, p. 116.

13. J.H. Barnes and H. Lucas, "Positive discrimination in education, individuals, groups and institutions", in T. Leggatt, (Ed) Social Theory and Survey Research, Sage, 1974, p.56.

14. D. Herbert, "Urban education, problems and policies", in D. Herbert and R. Johnston, Social Areas in Cities, op. cit., p. 153.

15. M. Rutter, N. Madge, "Cycles of disadvantage", HEB, 1977, p. 139.

16. R. Berthoud, p. 117.

17. R. King, Social Class, educational attainment and provision: an LEA study, Policy and Politics, 3, 1, 1974.

18. Department of the Environment, "Change or decay", HMSO, 1977, p. 158.

19. D. Byrne, B. Williamson, B. Fletcher, "The poverty of education", Robertson, 1975.

20. An extreme example of this is the American Heber project, focussed on an inner city tract in Milwaukee. Intensive contacts between the child, two teachers and the parents lasted from very early infancy through to the sixth year on a five day week, 12 months a year basis. The study has noted marked intellectual progression for both children, and as an offshoot, for the parents. See, M. Rutter, N. Madge, Cycles of disadvantage, HEB, 1977, pp. 135-7.

21. J. Simmie, "Citizens in conflict", Hutchinson, 1974, p. 218.

22. Ibid, p. 218.

23. R. Berthoud, "The disadvantages of inequality", PEP, 1976, p. 130.

24. CDP, "The costs of industrial change", CDP 1977, p. 36.

25. J. Hill, "The psychological impact of unemployment", New Society, 19 January 1977, p. 120.

26. M. Colledge, "Young people and work", Department of Employment Gazette, 85, 12, 1978.

27. Department of the Environment, "Inner London", HMSO 1977, p. 82.

28. R. Berthoud, "The disadvantages of inequality", PEP, 1976, p. 63.

29. J. Bradshaw, "Poverty trap", New Society, 8 December 1977, p. 520.

30. W.W. Daniel and E. Stilgoe, "Where are they now?": a follow-up study of the unemployed, PEP Report 572, 1977.

31. Department of the Environment, "Inner London", HMSO 1977, p. 98.

32. E. Burney, "Housing on trial", OUP, 1967.

33. J.A. Rex, "The Sociology of a zone in transition", in Readings in Urban Sociology, Ed. R.E. Pahl, Pergamon, 1968.

34. J.G. Davies, "The evangelistic bureaucrat", Tavistock, 1972.

35. F. Gray, "Selection and allocation in Council housing", Transactions, Institute of British Geographers, NS 1, 1, 1976, p. 34-46.

36. A.M. Kirby and S.E. Jeffs, "Management or managerialism - a view of the Housing Policy Consultative Document", Paper submitted to the Department of the Environment, November 1977. Information on Derby taken from A. Mansey, Allocation of council housing - the results, a case study in Derby C.B., Mimeo, Reading.

37. R.E. Pahl, Whose city?, Penguin Books, Harmondsworth, 1975.

38. CDP, "Whatever happened to council housing?", CDP, 1976.

39. Department of the Environment, Change or decay, HMSO, 1977, p. 52.

40. H. Bird, "Residential mobility and preference patterns in the public sector of the housing market", Transactions Institute of British Geographers, NS 1, 1, 1976, pp. 20-33.

41. Department of the Environment, "Inner London", HMSO, 1977, p. 124. It is interesting to note that the Lambeth Study makes the following observation about the cycle of deprivation: "in the characteristic diagrams portraying this cycle, the assumption is made that low income usually leads to households living in bad housing. Our study suggests that on the contrary, income poverty and housing deprivation are not strongly associated with each other", (p. 64). This statement is contentious because, a) no-one wants to suggest that all households with low incomes finish up in deprived circumstances, and b) because the analysis leading up to the conclusion is fallacious. One cannot make inductions from a small biased sample of those already in the inner city, and transfer the conclusions to society as a whole. To take a colourful example, if we were to correlate performance at high jumping with the individual's height, we must take a full sample of heights. We could take a large number of midgets, and find that there is little correlation between height and height jumped. Some at, say, three feet tall can jump a certain height, some slightly shorter can jump a little higher. This does not mean there

is no correlation <u>in general</u>: a six-footer will always jump higher than a three-footer. Similarly, those on £2,000 p.a. will always have a worse chance in the housing market than those on £10,000 p.a., regardless of the absence of any relationship between variations in housing for all those on £2,000 p.a.

42. A.A. Nevitt, "Housing, taxation and subsidies", Nelson, 1966, p. 141.

43. H.J. Gans, "Urbanisation and suburbanism as ways of life", in A.M. Rose, "<u>Human behaviour and social processes</u>", RKP, 1962, pp. 625-648.

44. Ibid, p. 628.

45. D.T. Herbert, "Social deviance in the city: a spatial perspective", in D. Herbert and R.J. Johnston, "<u>Social areas in cities</u>", Vol. 2, Wiley, 1976, pp. 89-121.

46. J. Shepherd, J. Westaway, T. Lee, "<u>A social atlas of London</u>", Oxford, 1974, p. 94. The component referred to within the quote is a statistical method of relating variables that occur together in some places and not in others. The method is discussed in an introductory fashion by J.B. Goddard and A.M. Kirby, "<u>An introduction to factor analysis</u>", Norwich, 1976.

47. D.M. Smith, "The geography of social well-being", McGraw-Hill, 1973, p. 48.

48. Department of the Environment, "<u>Unequal city</u>", HMSO, 1977, pp. 31, 32.

49. M. Rutter and N. Madge, "<u>Cycles of disadvantage</u>", HEB, 1977, p. 219.

50. Ibid, p. 220.

51. Ibid, p. 223.

52. D. Herbert, "Social deviance in the city: a spatial perspective", op cit, p. 100.

53. Department of the Environment, "<u>Change or decay</u>", HMSO, 1977, p. 163. The study referenced is that of H.J. Parker, "<u>View from the boys: downtown adolescents</u>", David and Charles, 1974.

54. R.E. Pahl, "Spatial and social constraints in the inner city", <u>Geographical Journal</u> 141, 1975, pp. 386-7.

55. Department of the Environment, "<u>Inner London</u>", HMSO, 1977, p. 87.

56. D. Perman, "Cublington, a blueprint for resistance", Bodley Head, 1973.

57. J.G. Davies, "<u>The evangelistic bureaucrat</u>", Tavistock, 1972.

58. J.R. Lambert, "Housing class and community action in a redevelopment area", in C. Lambert and D. Weir, op. cit.

59. Department of the Environment, "Change or decay", HMSO, 1977, p. 167.

60. See for example J. Grant, "The politics of urban transport planning", Friends of the Earth, 1977. Grant makes the subtle point that protesting about the line of a road only enforces the necessity of a road at all. It is necessary, for success, to argue against a road at any price, as happened in Nottingham.

61. Department of the Environment, "Change or decay", HMSO, 1977, p. 176.

62. P. Ambrose and B. Colenutt, "The property machine", Penguin Books, Harmondsworth, 1975, p. 102.

63. D. Donnison, "Micro-politics of the city", in D. Donnison and D. Eversley, op cit, p. 387.

64. Urban social movements are identified by the Urban Sociology school, and relate to the growth of political consciousness in threatened communities; the most accessible references are to be found in C.G. Pickvance, "Urban sociology", Tavistock, 1976.

65. Department of the Environment, "Change or decay", HMSO, 1977, p. 177.

66. Department of the Environment, "Unequal city", HMSO, 1977, p. 294.

67. C. Cockburn, "The local state", Pluto Press, 1977, pp. 7-87.

68. CDP, "Gilding the ghetto", CDP, 1977, p. 5.

69. Ibid, p. 55.

Chapter Five

A C T I O N - O R P E N D I N G ?

INTRODUCTION

In some spheres, social science has a good deal of
influence. Some of the major planning issues of this
decade have drawn on the brains of economists, geographers,
political scientists and traffic engineers, and there
seems some evidence that their views hold credence
amongst decision-makers. However, these issues were
mainly specific ones: where to build a new airport,
how to decide where to put a new trunk road [1] Moreover,
the academics were using tools, which produced plans,
policies and opinions in the end, but which were themselves 'objective' and 'scientific'.

Urban problems do not fit into this mould, because
there are no statistical or mathematical models that
can tell us how to deal with the inner city. [2] In
consequence, as Ray Pahl suggests:

> "those in central and local government who sponsor
> research may well be feeling cheated and irritated.
> They were urged to find out more about the urban
> system before they fiddled about with it. So
> funds were made available to set up the Centre
> for Environmental Studies, to produce large,
> government-sponsored regional planning studies and
> to support the Greater London Development Plan.
> Yet when (these) helped to show the limits of
> planners' powers, no-one responsible for
> determining policy was made particularly happy.
> It is one thing to sponsor a research programme
> into a specific social problem which is particularly
> intractable; it is quite another to acknowledge
> that the problem area is a product of a situation

where the majority feel well-off and do not feel
much concern to redistribute their modest level
of affluence to the poor. <u>*Government departments*</u>
<u>*have to assume that solutions can be found within*</u>
<u>*the economic and political system broadly as it*</u>
<u>*is.*</u>*" (my emphasis)*

The inner city problem, as it has been rehearsed here,
is not going to be easily solved, because as Pahl
points out, much of the present analysis of the situation
starts off from the assumption that the capitalist mode
of production is the fundamental problem, and that the
inner areas are simply a living testament to that fact.
Clearly governments can invoke no planning strategy
that takes as its first premise such an assumption.

In consequence, when we come now to look at ways
in which new inner area strategies might be developed,
we do not find simply choices between Plan A and Plan B,
(to build at Windscale or not to build, an airport at
Stansted or an airport at Foulness). Instead we find
structural analyses, economic analyses, socially-based
analyses, each with its related policy, and each with
proponents (and critics). I see four *main* solutions
to the problem in hand, and these are summarised in
Figure Two. (Other analyses, and other solutions
exist, and these will be discussed in passing).

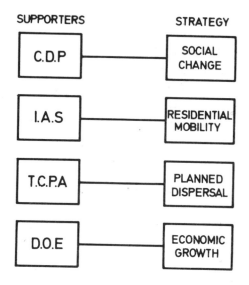

Figure Two: Inner city strategies and proponents:
for details see text.

The four strategies can be seen to emphasise very
different aspects of the problem. As I have just
outlined, a strong school of thought regards major
social and economic change as a necessary precursor to
a removal of inner city deprivation: although they are
by no means the only supporters, the Community
Development Project has been prominent in the promotion
of this line.

The second strategy is just one aspect of the
package of recommendations produced by the Inner Area
Studies Final Reports, namely a 'relaxation' of the
housing market, in order to allow households greater
movement between and within sectors, and in consequence,
greater geographical mobility. This recommendation is
stressed by the more sensitive of the Final Reports,
and is discussed in detail by the Lambeth Study. As
we shall see, this portion of the package has not been

taken on board with any enthusiasm by the Government:
instead emphasis has been placed upon economic
revitalisation by policy advisors within the Department
of the Environment, and this interest can be seen
clearly in the 1977 "Policy for the Inner Cities"
White Paper.

The fourth major strategy is very different in
tone and intent from the others, concentrating as it
does upon population and employment *dispersal*, rather
than a concentration of resources within the inner
areas. This line, which has of course, as New Towns
policy, been the past Government strategy, is still
widely supported - the Town and Country Planning
Association is to the forefront of informed opinion on
the matter.

Of the four approaches, the first clearly adopts
a very different standpoint from the rest, in so far
as it concludes that there can be no real planning
solution to the inner city problem. This is obviously
a stance that has to be come to terms with, and it is
thus with the question of social change that we begin.

"Development into Decline"

To isolate the processes at work within a city is
no easy task: however this task pales visibly alongside the problem of accounting for the decline of the
small firm, or the extension of suburban housing out
into the rural-urban fringe. To say that greenfield
sites are more attractive to industry, or that the
structure of the housing market makes home purchase
a better financial investment than renting, is simply
to consider again symptoms of deeper economic, social
and political processes. More to the point, some
analyses, particularly the Marxist one, would not
separate the economic from the social or political
spheres, but would see the last two realms as a product

of the first.

When we come to look specifically at the inner city,
the manifest decline has been attributed to nothing less
than the structural changes being undergone by the
capitalist system. In the very simplest of terms, this
change relates to the form of capital in existence
within society. Over time, the amounts of capital naturally
increase, and these are switched increasingly from
industrial to fixed investments like buildings - either
office blocks, or speculative homes for purchase.[4]

The study of Peter Ambrose and Bob Colenutt has
already been introduced: in it, they show how *"the
interests of the land and capital owners are ranged
against those of the would-be user. One is acting in
accordance with an economic imperative and wants the
highest possible financial return. The other needs
housing or some other socially important facility at
the lowest possible cost. Wants against needs, owners
against users."*[5] The ways in which this conflict of
interest is manifest are varied: to return to the case
of Southwark, (see Chapter Four), the decision made
by the Borough to both permit and encourage the development of office building sparked off a round of heady
speculation in the 1967-72 period. Proximity to Central
London, rising property prices due to a shortage of
office space, and a surplus of 'new' money like pension
funds all fuelled a round of investment in Southwark. A
typical process was to take over a local firm, not
for its economic worth, but simply for the land it
occupied. The business is wound up, the workers made
redundant, the premises demolished, and the land either
built upon, or resold for building purposes - the classic
asset-stripping method. In the 1967-72 period, something
like 17,000 jobs in the Borough were lost. Further, as
we have seen, the new jobs tend not to be available to
those displaced, because the skills do not tally: the

20,000 office jobs created go therefore to commuters
rather than the local population. On the other side
of the coin, deals worth between £70 million and £100
million were made, almost all of which was profit since
no development gains tax was due at that time.[6]

Naturally, these speculative developments do not
happen in a vacuum. Both Central and Local Governments
have allowed offices to be built. The role of the
central agency in allowing office developments to be
incorporated within local plans is obscure, given the
promotion, at the same time, of schemes to *decentralise*
office use out of London. It seems likely however that
the financial question is important: local authorities
have experienced a loss of independence resulting from
a declining importance of rate revenue in their spending.[7]
Local government is thus keen to bring in new buildings
that can be rated, whilst Central authority is happy to
reduce, or at least hold constant the amounts of cash
that have to go towards supporting local services via
the rate support grant.

Of course, London tends to be a special case in
any argument about the national trends within the
economy. As I have already suggested, in the inner
areas of centres like Bradford or Newcastle an
apparently more straightforward process of industrial
decline is at work. The demise of ship-building and
textile production is due to changing demands, and
strong competition from foreign competitors. Furthermore, there is also the question of increasing
rationalisation and consolidation within industry. The
American pattern of centralisation, take-over and then
overseas expansion is being repeated here. Stuart
Holland, economist and Labour Party advisor has talked
about the growth of a 'meso-economic' sector, which no
longer need obey the usual dictates of economic
necessity.[8] The firms that constitute this sector are

giants like ICI and Ford, who can dictate general price
levels in several countries. One result of their mode
of operation, suggests Holland, is an unwillingness
to invest in the regional areas which contain problem
centres like Newcastle and Glasgow: many of the
traditional incentives to transfer employment to the
Development Areas outside the South-East of England
are relatively unattractive to firms who can exploit
cheap labour in South Africa, or South Korea. Moreover,
the increasing trend towards take-over means that,
increasingly, fewer firms are responsible only to
themselves. Instead, businesses operating within the
Development Areas in general, and in the inner areas in
particular, face closure on the grounds of being
unprofitable, relative to the rest of the group holdings.
The CDP report several examples of national or
international firms rationalising their plant at
national scale, with particularly severe results for
core areas: e.g. the emphasis upon methane gas,
resulting in closure of many large town-gas works.
In Canning Town alone, this accounted for 5,000 workers
losing their jobs, whilst several other examples exist,
such as the changing location of the BICC cable group.
In Saltley (Birmingham), Leyland have continually
contracted their employment since the 1960's: *"the
workers of Saltley did not lose their jobs because
firms actually relocated. The jobs were eliminated as
the companies reinvested and directed their capital
towards concentrating production somewhere else"*.[9]

These changes assume an almost predictable pattern,
given the nature of economic pressures upon business.
It is however interesting to note that Government has
played its part too in inner city industrial decline.
Since the 1930's, emphasis has lain firmly upon *regional*
problems: large-scale pockets of unemployment. One of
the methods designed to overcome this was the provision

of attractive facilities in new, equally attractive
sites. These New Towns have, in the main, been very
successful in attracting employment and population,
as recent studies have shown.[10] In consequence, any
mobile industry has been attracted and channelled into
greenfield, rather than urban sites, (although as we
have seen, there has been less effect upon firms
already within the cores). Furthermore, firms
receiving aid from the National Enterprise Board are
becoming as ready to release labour as businesses
operative in the open market, as recent plans for
British Leyland illustrate. These then are the sort
of contexts within which inner city decay needs to
be considered. As the CDP observe however, Government
policy has been, so far, *"piecemeal"*, providing *"little
more than cosmetic treatment"*.

> *"At best they could only relieve or cover up
> the more obvious symptoms of urban decline. The
> root problems were well beyond their reach.
> Throughout, the urban programme has assumed
> that problems of poverty and deprivation in such
> areas could meaningfully be tackled without
> reference to the basic economic context."*[11]

If this then is the critical analysis, what of the policy
formulations? The CDP suggest that:

> *"The most relevant measures are not to be found
> in tinkering with housing or labour markets,
> nor with population dispersal policies, nor in
> the creation of special development agencies or
> regional assemblies - but with measures designed
> to control the activities of capital."*[12]

These measures are seen to include both public ownership
and indirect controls:

> *"the latter would (include) the take up of
> public controlling shareholdings in leading
> firms, the enforcement of planning agreements*

> *between government, unions and employers, and*
> *the right for unions to have information on*
> *the forward strategies of the large companies.*
> *Planning agreements...such as forward*
> *investment programmes, manning levels, job*
> *creation and location, technological*
> *development, export programmes, and pricing*
> *policies."*[13]

As a policy package, it is clear that this is
superficially attractive, not least in the wider
context of national development. Its connections
with the inner city problem remain tenuous however.
I see three main drawbacks.

The first relates to the extent of the interface
between industry and deprivation. I have tried to
show that the question is not one of unemployment. To
be fair, the CDP is keen to point out the nature of
many new inner city jobs: unskilled, long hours,
poorly-paid. However, there is a danger that
emphasising an employment solution to area-based
poverty will simply result in a proliferation of what
we may call in shorthand 'Grunwick-type' enterprises.

A related argument is the emphasis upon what is
essentially nationalised industry or nationally
accountable industry. It is becoming increasingly
obvious that the public sector is differentially
rewarded vis-a-vis the private sector, especially in
a period of wage restraint. If one is going to use a
Marxist type analysis. it seems a curious lacuna to
overlook the traditional view of the State as an agent
of capital, not as its opponent - in other words State
industry is just as prepared to pay low wages (in
hospitals for example) as any free-market employer.

The final argument relates to the possibility of
diminishing poverty via economic growth. The United
States has not achieved it: in any country, there is

likely to remain a group (or class) who are economically
weak. These individuals, (or groups such as Blacks,
or say Catholics, in Northern Ireland) will continue
to use inner city locations due to the housing question -
and economic revitalisation will not automatically
improve the supplies of services and housing. These
will still require the piecemeal reforms that have been
tried throughout the last decade.

I think that these problems expose the major
failing of the CDP analysis. It isolates capitalism
as a major culprit, and yet expects that changes can
be brought about within the basic, existing framework.
This seems inconsistent. Either capitalism should go,
to be replaced by an alternative economic system,[14] or
specific inner city solutions are sought within the
extant set-up. To aim however for economic reforms,
and hope that these will automatically aid inner urban
poverty, is too much an article of faith.

The ramifications of a revolutionary social,
political and economic change have yet to be thought
through. Let us therefore draw back from this analysis,
and investigate more specific policies operating
within the status quo.

"Dispersal and Balance"
A point heavily stressed in Chapter Four was
that within the housing market, all roads lead back
to the inner city for those living there. Significantly,
both the Liverpool and Lambeth Inner Area Studies place
some emphasis upon the institutional changes that are
necessary within the market to change this situation.
Essentially, there are two sorts of housing solution
possible: the first concentrates upon improving the
housing situation of those who want to remain within
the inner areas, whilst the second involves strategies
that allow those who wish to leave to do so.

The Liverpool Final Report argues that three changes
in the local authority housing sector are required:
these involve an extension of public responsibility,
the creation of a social needs policy, and an
improvement of the council transfer system.[15] The
first topic relates essentially to the types of
individuals and households who are at present given
little help by council housing: single persons, small
families without children, the mobile, for example.
Such groups are limited essentially to privately
rented accommodation, and much stress could be alleviated
by the provision of (public) furnished rooms and multiply-
occupied flats. Some Housing Associations are already
providing such flexible accommodation.

The existence of a social needs policy relates to
the desirability of extending and expanding the criteria
by which housing aid can be given: *"to the current medical
criteria might be added long-term unemployment; large
or single-parent families; a history of institutional
care; sub-tenanting or a risk of eviction"*.[16] Such a
policy would for example reduce the possibility of
families entering a recurrent cycle of homelessness,
short-life property, rent-arrears and further housing
stress, and eviction once more, by acting before the
homelessness came about.

The third proposal relates directly back to the
comments made earlier in relation to the delays found
within the council transfer process. Average waits of
several years clearly foster an inefficient use of
the housing stock. In order to overcome these delays,
the Liverpool report suggests greater liaison between
authorities to help inter-urban migration, plus a
willingness to allow more intra-urban moves. One
additional side-effect of such a policy would be the
eventual evacuation of hard-to-let estates, which would
in turn force the Housing Department to either improve

the dwellings and environment, or to demolish the
properties altogether.

The Lambeth study reiterates these policies,
whilst expressing them within the metropolitan context.
It stresses for example that council tenants in Inner
London Boroughs should have access to council property
in Outer London, and that more property should be built
in both Outer London and the green belt fringes. A
formal National Housing Allocations Pool is proposed
to aid longer moves.

More detailed changes are also outlined - that
both private and public rents should be allowed to
rise for example, in order to finance improvements
to property within both sectors. A wide range of
flexible strategies are also discussed: for instance,
that some tenants be encouraged to take up local
authority, index-linked mortgages. Similarly, housing
improvements in the private sector should be approved,
not on an area basis, but in terms of the standards
of the individual property. Finally there is a wide
package of measures, designed to improve the housing
situation of existing estates. Shops and nurseries
are proposed for the present, whilst future estates
should give greater attention to layout, and further
sorts of facilities. Emphasis upon tenant participation
is also recommended, as a means of reducing vandalism
and neglect. [17]

In themselves, these proposals are, with one or
two exceptions, satisfactory measures. They do however
concentrate upon the *public* sector as the answer to
inner city housing problems. This ignores the role
of the owner-occupied housing sector within the
market, a strange oversight considering that the latter
now accounts for over half the households in the country.
Investment in the inner areas will remain low until the
policy of red-lining disappears, and the savings of

numerous small Building Society investors stop flowing out to finance suburban purchasing.[18] Instead this cash should stay within the core, to fuel owner-occupation in situ. Although some observers worry about the subtle political motives behind owner-occupation, we may underline the fact that for some families, home purchasing can be as cheap as renting accommodation, due to the amount of tax-relief generally available.[19]

The question of subsidy also needs examination: it is clearly inequitable that building society mortgage relief should progressively increase with income, whilst, as we have already seen, private rental receives no formal subsidy. For this reason, proposals to actually increase both private and public sector rents seem a curious move, when the possibility exists to make profits on landlordism open to a lower rate of taxation. This would transfer the onus of improvement back to the pocket of the owner of the property, not the tenant.

Any policy package then that fails to come to terms with the home-ownership sector must be regarded as narrow. What is more worrying however is that the strategies outlined by the Final Reports overlook existing realities. As far as transfer systems are concerned, there is obviously much that needs doing (e.g. in terms of transfering records to computer systems). However the recent Housing Green Paper made no formal policy initiative on this score, beyond a vague suggestion that improvements be made.[20] Clearly, no National Housing Allocations Pool is in the pipeline. Moreover, an emphasis upon transfers faces a major problem in London, where the existence of numerous Boroughs makes a unified strategy difficult. The Lambeth Report's suggestions concerning *"co-ordinated allocation to facilitate migration from Inner to Outer*

London",[21] will never be ratified by the present GLC
Housing Committee. All building in Outer London has
been stopped, and all the 70,000 properties suitable
for sale will be offered to sitting tenants. Instead,
£36 million will be made available for home purchase in
Inner London, along with £5m for council property
improvement in the inner areas, and a similar sum for
housing associations. George Tremlett, chairman of
the GLC Housing Policy Committee, is on record as
saying that *"you cannot say that London is one city",*
and that there are *"separate communities, and they
should keep separate housing management identities."*
There will be, for the future at least, no more
"shuffling people about London".[22]

The whole question of transfers is in itself a
contentious one, simply because the needs of those
already in accommodation need to be balanced against
the needs of those trying to get into the local authority
sector for the first time. At a time of limited new
building, a concentration of energies upon transfer
policies can only work against those in privately
rented property, who are objectively in the greatest
housing need.

The Inner Area Studies have not really come to
grips with these types of issues. Nor have they faced
up to the question of Housing Department politics.
For example, is existing policy, which seems to operate
against households who are thought to be 'problems', to
be changed? Will all families be allowed to transfer,
without let or hindrance? It will be hard to change
the existing Housing Management ethos, which is
ruthlessly professional and based upon the requirements
of managing property, not sorting out social problems
or mopping up after the collapse of inner areas.[23] I
am similarly doubtful about the proposals designed to
increase tenant participation in the running of estates.

In general, participation usually means an opening of
channels, so that professional wishes can be transfered
more effectively to the client, rather than vice-versa.[24]
Where tenant participation has been tried already, these
findings are repeated:

> "*tenant influence on decisions and council
> policy was found to be uncertain, small, and
> connected with the willingness of the councils,
> and officers, to be influenced. The discrepancy
> between the political reason for participation,
> in giving tenants more power over decision making,
> and the systems set up which were not designed
> to achieve this, belied to a certain extent the
> commitment of the councils to the idea of
> participation*".[25]

To summarise, the question of residential mobility
is an important one: social mobility (in the context
of the inner areas, at any rate) is difficult to
achieve without geographical mobility, and this in
turn needs changes within the overall housing market
structure. Of importance here is the fact that housing
can be used as an agent of social change, and that
housing policy need not concentrate solely upon bricks
and mortar. One interesting point to be noted within
the Liverpool and Lambeth studies is in fact the low
importance attached to the improvement, rehabilitation
and redevelopment aspects of housing. Both reports develop
the theme that policies such as HAAs produce an over-
concentration of investment which leaves many properties
overlooked. The net results, expressed in terms of
the heavy demands placed upon financial and personnel
resources, is thus disappointing. In contrast, the
Birmingham Final Report advocates a reduction of new
council house building on the outer estates, using the
savings "*to accelerate GIA and HAA programmes, and
where appropriate, inner area redevelopment to a firm*

and realistic timetable."[26] Whilst it is perhaps
possible to argue for such a policy on economic
grounds (i.e. the costs of improvement versus the
costs of new-build strategies), we are still left with
the question of a poor inner city environment, and
bad job prospects, unaffected by simple housing
rehabilitation, a point that the Report is not unaware
of: *"if we provide better housing but the people who
live in these houses have no jobs and no access to
education, recreation, shopping and other services and
have no mobility, the effort is largely wasted".*[27]

The Small Heath study, like the other Reports has
specific recommendations on employment, which we shall
examine presently. However, these apart, we are still
left with a package offering 'more of the same': greater
expenditure upon education, welfare, and community
self-determination. Although the "social change"
argument may be over-ambitious in its scope, we must
still confront the conclusion that the problems of the
cores do not all begin there, and that area-based
remedies are unlikely to deal with other than the
symptoms. Greater mobility seems necessary, although
the political will to achieve this is yet to be seen.

This section has concentrated essentially upon
residential mobility within a housing market framework.
However, migration can be approached as part of a
planned dispersal policy, itself incorporated into a
regional or even national planning framework. It is
to this that we now turn.

"Decentralisation versus improvement"

The policy of urban decentralisation is probably
Britain's oldest planning strategy. Its antecedents
date back to the early thinkers in physical planning,
like Ebenezer Howard: the latter's influential work
"Garden Cities of Tomorrow", appeared late in the

nineteenth century, but was already promoting an
evacuation of the crowded industrial centres.[28]

Although conditions in the twentieth century city
have, in absolute terms at least, improved, it is
essentially since the second world war that these ideas
have been translated into action. The New Towns Act
of 1946 represented an answer to a spectrum of problems:
physical overcrowding, urban decay accelerated by six
years of warfare, a strategic urge to make the major
centres less of a concentrated target in an atomic age,
plus the pressures upon rural land caused by suburban
encroachment. Succeeding generations of New Towns, and
overspill Expanded Towns have thus been built to
accept 'surplus' population from the conurbations, to
provide a modern focus for light industry, and to
take pressure off "green belt" land trying to hold the
towns and cities in.

It should be said straightaway that the New Towns
represent a surprisingly successful planning strategy:
since the pioneers like Crawley and Stevenage, something
like 930,000 people have moved in; 904,000 jobs have
been created, all for an outlay of £1,332 million. The
housing is generally of a high standard, unemployment
is usually low (although New Towns are as susceptible
to regional unemployment as any urban area - Peterlee
has over 11% out of work at the present time for example),
and the facilities like schools, modern and purpose-
built.

Despite this success, or more probably because of
it, Government has cut back on New Town investment.
Already the last site to be designated, (the ill-fated
Stonehouse, outside Glasgow) has been scrapped. As
we have already discussed, the reasons for this are not
hard to find - the New Towns are open to charges of
causing inner city decline. More importantly however,
demographic statistics suggest a dramatic falling away

of population growth towards the end of the decade,
with the result that new building to relieve congestion
may not be required.

Peter Shore's decisions have not ended the New
Towns versus Inner Cities debate: indeed, as Robert
Coursey's recent study shows, his action has fuelled
the discussion.[29] The Government plan has, for example,
been heavily criticised by the Town and Country Planning
Association, not to mention the New Towns themselves.
Four areas of contention exist.

The first argument suggests that it is a chimera
to rob Peter to pay Paul in this way. As the 1976-7
Rate Support Grant figures show, it is possible to
finance the urban areas without touching New Town
funds. More to the point, the cash is useful to the
town Commissioners, but of only marginal use to the
inner areas - £350 million per year would not go very
far.

Secondly, it is a mistake to assume that building
should depend upon population projections. A far more
dynamic factor within the national context is the
change to ever-smaller households, setting up younger,
and staying independent longer. Single persons, and
an increasing number of elderly couples will continue
to place pressure upon the housing stock. This is not
to forget either that the latter is also continually
ageing, and in need of replacement.

Thirdly, the New and Expanded Towns are seen as
a planning achievement: certainly, the numbers of
visitors who scrutinise some of the older settlements
on behalf of overseas planning authorities suggests
that our view of the Garden City movement is perhaps
different from foreign views of our creation.
Superficially at least, there exists a good deal of
social mixing within any one development and as we
might expect, indicators of stress like vandalism

and rent arrears tend to be low.

Fourthly, there is doubt as to the wisdom of trying to channel industry back into the cities, when some activities would prefer to locate in greenfield sites. It would clearly be a hollow victory to restrict industrial investment in the New Towns, if the net result was an overall loss of investment to the country as a whole.

Opposition to the ideas of decentralisation operates on a rather subtle level. It does not normally argue that New Towns are a phenomenon that should be in some way "stopped". Rather, it argues that decentralisation out to overspill areas will never solve the inner city problem, and consequently emphasis must be placed upon a coherent strategy to solve the latter. Essentially, we can muster three types of argument that relate to this point.

To begin with, let us return briefly to the question of New Towns causing inner city problems. Ray Pahl has written that:

> *"attempts to minimize spatial inequality very*
> *often have latent consequences the reverse of*
> *those expected. The British New Town Policy*
> *may provide a good example. The channelling*
> *of resources to skilled-manual-worker and*
> *green-field sites took away capital and*
> *professional expertises from inner city*
> *environments and the less-skilled workers."*[30]

This is a little wide of the mark. Whilst it is interesting to conjecture that inner city planning strategies produce such bad results because the New Town Corporations attract the most able planners, it is not correct to say that green-field sites are attracting capital away from the inner areas in large amounts. As we have seen in Chapter Three, most firms in the core seem to go out of business, rather than

migrate. Even those that move tend not to take their
workers with them: (if in fact some process of migration
were in evidence, this could perhaps be used in support
of the decentralisation issue). However, as the Lambeth
study indicates, only about a third of migrants
arriving in the New and Expanded Towns come from Inner
London: *"since the towns attract modern firms, and
since most such firms are in Outer London, Inner
Londoner are unlikely to move out in this way"*.[31]
Until the New Towns change their regulations, to allow
unskilled workers to move in without first possessing
a job, this is unlikely to change, suggests the Report.
Interestingly, the Lambeth study also states that
these towns are never likely to offer major amounts of
low grade employment, and that the strategy of actually
allowing a level of unemployment more typical of the
national average should be encouraged in order to reduce
the levels in the core areas.

The major weakness of the decentralisation argument
is manifest in the second issue, namely the question
of residual populations. Simply, it is a pious hope
that overspill can decant away all the residents from
the cores. There will always be a residual, and of
course for them it is quite possible that conditions
would be relatively poorer than at present, as the
population thresholds needed to support services such
as clinics are passed; (this in turn relates to the
rate support grant question, which is considered
shortly). The residual will remain for various
reasons. Some may not wish to leave their communities;
many will not simply be able to move within the housing
market. Even those who are mobile may not have a
marketable skill to make a move worthwhile. Economists
have recently argued that in the inner city, *"high
rates of unemployment and associated problems do
constitute an economic problem in that from the point of*

view of the economy, these are under-utilised resources". They continue to argue that decentralisation may have made some firms in the inner city relatively unprofitable, but more importantly, that

> *"council housing provides a substantial*
> *encouragement to unemployment in inner areas*
> *as the jobs move out. Once in low rent*
> *council housing in an inner city area a*
> *household would suffer a marked decline in*
> *real income if it moved because of the*
> *virtual impossibility of obtaining similar*
> *low-rent accommodation elsewhere."*[31]

They continue to argue that *"the most sensible policy now would be to abandon the present policy of decentralisation to new and to expanding towns; the building of council houses in areas of labour surplus should be discontinued, as should green belt controls... Such policy changes would give an impetus to development in outer urban areas".*[32] This the authors see to be of potential advantage to inner city residents, as it would provide accessible employment.

The problem with this novel solution, (which of course rather overlooks the political question of siting new industry in close proximity to suburban housing) is that it ignores the issue of providing for the remaining population. This is a double-edged problem, firstly because expenditure is high (as on, for example, council house provision) and secondly because of the weak tax-base. Local authority finance can be examined under three main headings: the balance of domestic, as opposed to industrial rate-payers within a district, the rateable value per head of population, and the needs of the local authority (i.e. the proportions of 'at risk' populations such as shared households, single parent families, unemployed workers and so on). Collectively these 'domestic',

'resources' and 'needs' elements constitute the Rate
Support Grant, which now provides over half of local
government spending from central funds. The drawback
with RSG provision is that whilst the inner areas do
well on the 'needs' allowance, they do badly on
'resources', which overestimates the amounts of
highly rated office property in many central business
districts. Special "clawback" provision has to be
made. Even so, we tend to find that at the end of the
day, inner area authorities still have higher penny
rate demands to make upon their proportionately poorer
populations.[33] Moreover, this really is felt by that
population, because inner city populations are very
bad at claiming their due rate rebates. Nationally,
Bournemouth has the highest level of take-up with over
a quarter of all residents receiving rebates: Hackney,
on the other hand, scoring extremely highly on any
scale of deprivation, has both almost the lowest
national take-up, and higher rates than many other
urban areas.

All in all then, decentralisation can only, it
seems, lead to serious financial problems resulting
from a need to service a diminished, but permanent
inner city population. As Coursey points out, the
problem lies with the fact that *"it advocates have
perhaps created the impression that its decentralisation is
an end itself"*, resulting in a one-pronged strategy
where perhaps two were required: *"it is to practical
measures towards the completion of the process of
transformation of the inner areas set in motion by
urban decentralisation, without the intervention of
Nemesis, that attention must be concentrated"*.[34]

This observation brings us back to positive
discrimination for the inner city, the last of the
four policy initiatives that I have identified.

"Radical Economic Policies"

Government has recently declared its hand with regard to the core areas with the production of the 1977 White Paper, and the 1978 Inner Urban Areas Bill. Whilst these have some comments to make concerning health, education, transport and the social services, the thrust of the discussion and policy proposals is firmly upon employment and industry: *"the decline in the economic fortunes of the inner areas lies at the heart of the problem."*[35]

The present Government is keen to emphasise a long term commitment to inner area provision: the budget for the Urban Programme is increased to £125m per annum, for example. The most important change of policy relates to the creation of the Partnership schemes, whereby Central Government has come to the aid of selected Local Authorities where deprivation is thought to be particularly serious. The Partnerships, and their intended finances, are shown below:

TABLE 10:   INNER CITY PARTNERSHIPS AND
PROPOSED EXPENDITURE 1978-9

Authority	*Aid (£m)*
Docklands	£3.50
London:Lambeth	1.00
Hackney/Islington	1.75
Liverpool	2.50
Manchester/Salford	2.50
Birmingham	2.50
Newcastle/Gateshead	1.75

Within the Partnership areas, cash will be available to assist small businesses to purchase land and improve buildings. Grants of £1000 will be available for construction work, and 90% mortgages for land purchase.

For the future, these types of aid will become
consolidated within Industrial Improvement Areas,
where authorities will be able to provide advance
factories to attract migratory industry. The first
such area has recently been declared under the Tyne-
Wear Act (1976) in Pelaw, Gateshead, where six factory
sites are to be built.

In the wider context, the White Paper also hopes
that both existing firms, and new small businesses,
can be accommodated in the cores. Interest is also
expressed in liason with the Location of Offices
Bureau to maintain the building of a few speculative
office developments, particularly within Inner London.

As a package, the shift of responsibility for
'Urban Aid' from the Home Office to the Department of
the Environment has produced a necessary realignment
of emphasis from social, to social and economic issues.
The extent to which the Inner Areas Bill will lead to
any noticeable improvement in inner city conditions is
however debateable. Home improvements are not quick,
but the building and leasing of factories is even
slower. Equally, the amounts of cash on offer are
small, and concentrated in a limited number of centres.
Although many of the smaller urban centres have inner
city problems (note the uptake of HAA provision, for
example), they will not, for the present at least, have
access to these industrially-based funds.

On the other hand, long-sighted cynics may
question whether small firms, perhaps prone to operating
on Grunwick-lines in order to maximise profitability,
will make a great deal of impact, not only upon male
unemployment, but the problem of low incomes generally.
As we have seen, office-building will certainly *not*
provide a demand for unskilled workers.

If we return to the economic analysis quoted
briefly in the last section, emphasis was placed upon

a continued policy of limited dispersal. In a
discussion of the desirability of attracting industry
back to the cores, the authors note that:

> *"the resources required to attract much*
> *employment back into the inner cities would*
> *be very substantial. They would have to be*
> *sufficient to counteract the marked decline in*
> *the profitability of inner city locations for*
> *firms. The arguments against employment*
> *subsidies for inner cities are the same as those*
> *against general employment subsidies; their*
> *benefits are largely illusory and the jobs*
> *created are likely to be at the cost of jobs*
> *elsewhere in the economy."*[36]

This question of profitability is all-important,
especially when we place inner area strategies back in
a regional context. Despite the apparent success of
regional policy, it has taken much time and heavy
monetary investment; (in the North-East, estimates are
as high as £16,000 per job created). If generally
unattractive Development Area sites are to be replaced
by even more narrowly defined sites for assistance,
mostly within the inner areas, as some suggest,[37] then
we could foresee *increased* investment of public funds
in job creation, with *poorer* results for regional
unemployment as a whole. Furthermore, the question of
London is anomalous here. One important stratagem
within regional policy is the limitation of industrial
development and expansion within the capital: yet one
of the most forceful recommendations of the Lambeth
study is that all restrictions on industrial location
within London should be scrapped.[38] London's gain
here would however be other inner cities' loss.

In the final analysis, it is, I think difficult to
be optimistic about these long-term palliatives.
Those who applaud regional development policies have

not come to terms with the types of industry attracted
(frequently branch plants), the nature of the work
(frequently poorly skilled, usually poorly paid), and
the type of workers involved (often 'surplus' female
labour). As the CDP observe:

> *"declining areas have little chance of being
> regenerated again. There is so little mobile
> industry at present that a successful 'work to
> the workers' policy is nothing more than a
> liberal utopian dream."*[39]

The problem rests of course with them offering an
alternative, other than socialist utopian dreams:

> *"While the government invents ever more 'special'
> programmes, it abandons the very policies that
> might really begin to cure the problems of the
> inner cities and older declining areas...measures
> designed to control the activities of capital.
> Now is the time to organise to achieve these
> aims; to acquire the political thrust so that
> measures can be formulated and implemented which
> will begin to control investment in the social
> interest, to produce a socially rational
> distribution of industry."*[40]

As I have already suggested however such policies are
outside the scope of contemporary practical politics.
A much more familiar picture has already been painted:

> *"of course, far more likely is a policy that is
> both expensive and ineffectual. Resources will
> be steered into inner cities, via rate support
> grant and special block grants, which will then
> support further inflated building projects,
> designed to keep the municipal bureaucracies in
> business. Vast sums will go on grants and loans
> and infrastructure to attract large-scale industry,
> which will either ignore them or use them to build
> automated factories which will actually reduce*

> employment. *Physical planners, whose whole
> training and experience has been in negative
> control of physical development, will be
> pressed into an area - the encouragement of
> entrepreneurship - for which they have no
> qualifications and no penchant."*[41]

For 'large-scale industry' read 'small firms', for
'reduce employment' read 'offer barely any employment',
and this is, I think, essentially correct.

Towards a Conclusion

It may seem an easy task to end a chapter on
policy initiatives, aimed at improving the lot of
over three million people, by simply concluding that
there is no policy package that will work. This is, of
course, a negation of the fruits of many concerned
researchers, not to mention the whole planning ethos.
Nonetheless, the problem of the inner cities is
essentially insoluble within the context of the present
social structure.

This lesson will be the last one to be learnt by
policy makers: not necessarily because the argument
is unpalatable, but rather because it is simply counter-
intuitive. How can a problem which involved such
identifiable groups as blacks, in such definable
locations as inner cities, involve strategies other
than applying aid to the most affected areas? It
seems commonsense that if people live in poor housing,
then those homes should be bulldozed down and the
people moved away. If, ten years later, there are
still poor houses, then it makes sense to try something
different, and to patch them up instead. If children
do badly at school, then better schooling is to be
provided; if services are poor, then better management
should be devised. And if unemployment is high, then
jobs must be created.

It is futile to blame Government and Local Authorities for their course of action. It is only just coming clear to researchers that society's faults can be reflected in space, just as much as environmental problems can impinge on society. This is of course the key. The inner cities are not problematic in themselves. They simply reflect wider tensions. This has been found again and again within the USA. The ghettoes are poor environments, with poor job opportunities. An apparent solution is to provide bus systems so that Blacks can travel out to suburban work-places. This fails miserably, because the ghetto employment problem is not one of location, but simply a reflection of the place of the ethnic minorities in the labour market.

This is really quite obvious. In many situations, we accept that there is a great deal wrong with 'the system'. Over the last century, the feminist movement has attacked the labour market, the political system, the academic hierarchy, in order to right its grievances - high rates of unemployment, prejudice, poor pay, unskilled labour and so on. This attack has even been taken up by Government, resulting in legislation. This happened of course because there are women everywhere - in inner cities, outer cities, rural areas, New Towns, all experiencing the same problem. There is no spatial concentration with particular deprivation. Yet had there been female ghettoes, it seems likely that area based policies would have been levied: not housing improvement perhaps, but special compensatory wages within these particular concentrations.

It is this confusion of the people, and the areas in which they live, that has negated all inner city policy. The next emphasis must be not upon *areas* of deprivation: after decades of spaceless planning, this has suddenly become "a spatial encumbrance". Instead,

policy should address itself to the at-risk *population*.
By ignoring their spatial concentration, their needs
will emerge into clear focus. The West Indians need
a social climate within which they do not require a
community for physical protection, as seems the case in
places like Wolverhampton.[42] The Race Relations Act
is one approach to this: positive discrimination in
the job market may on the other hand be unwittingly
deleterious. Asians require, in turn, encouragement
to organise their own salvation: to buy their own
houses, shops and businesses. The extent, however to
which their sorties into landlordism will increasingly
attract the opprobrium attached to other races engaged
in this in the past remains open for debate.

The Blacks are an obvious and visible concentration.
Alongside them we have, as we have seen, less visible
groups like single-parent families and the elderly.
Here, the needs are more modest, and have been identified
by the Inner Area Studies: better accommodation,
proper support facilities, and in the final analysis,
a lack of discrimination within job and housing
markets. Different again are the unskilled: the
solution lies not with trying to attract work to them,
for this only reinforces the problems of being unskilled -
after all, all these workers have to offer is their
time, and lots of it. Their needs are instead intensive
training or re-training, in order that they can find a
place within the economy as it stands: this too is a
suggestion that remains buried within the Inner Area
Reports.

Encompassing these admittedly long-term aims (the
investment required for educational improvement and
industrial retraining alone would be enormous) is the
question of mobility, and behind that the housing market.
The only thing that all the inner city groups have in
common is their weakness within the housing market.

It is the latter that causes them to be spatially
concentrated, but it is also the market that will be
the most difficult aspect of the situation to change.
The question of political will is something I have
touched upon several times. There is no will to
restructure the housing market, to remove the subsidies
for the wealthy, to open up the public sector to those
least able to help themselves, and to facilitate
movement between and within local authorities once the
latter is achieved. At all levels, from the Party
political to the professional, there are impediments
to change. More worrying however, is the possibility
that the falling birth-rate will be used as an excuse
for shelving the inner city housing problem indefinitely.
In just the same way that declining numbers of children
have been used as a rationale by Local Education
Authorities to cut down on the numbers of teaching staff
employed (as opposed to using the situation as an
opportunity to improve teacher-pupil ratios), it is
possible that an overall reduction in pressure on the
housing stock *"too many homes chasing too few people"*,[43]
will also lead to a reduction in investment. Attempts
are perenially made to argue that there is no national
housing shortage, in so far as the number of dwellings
already exceeds the number of households. A fall in the
population of London in excess of one million adults
by 1991 will undoubtedly lead to less investment in
home improvement and a reduced rate of new local
authority building. This would be an arithmetically
logical conclusion, repeated throughout the country to
varying degrees. It ignores however the fact that a
significant proportion of our existing stock is in
poor condition, either as a result of design faults
(tower blocks), or sheer old-age. There will only be
a surplus of property if these substandard dwellings
remain within the equation, and indeed the concentration

of these types of homes in the inner cities would make
their demolition impossible, in so far as the virtual
evacuation of most inner areas would be involved.
Although this would solve the whole inner city problem,
the solution is so total, not to say draconian, as to
be impracticable.

Whatever logistical changes occur within the
housing market, I can see no ultimate end to the sorts
of problems facing those at the end of the housing
queue. Falling population pressure upon privately
rented accommodation will be offset by the continual
ageing of the housing stock and the removal from the
market of the poorest dwellings. Falling numbers
within the population at large will still leave a
demand for council housing that exceeds the supply,
even if the undesirable inner area properties remain
in use, due to the reduction in building that is almost
certain to occur. Nor will owner-occupation become any
cheaper: a far more likely outcome is that prices
within the sector will rise only slowly, allowing some
households to purchase a second home, and others to
enter home-ownership earlier in the family-cycle. In
all cases then, the question of mobility for the inner
city dweller remains unanswered. As the CDP has
observed in vigorous terms:

> *"whatever they do, the name of the game is*
> *still the same: private profit. For 200 years*
> *it has failed to provide good houses for everyone.*
> *It doesn't now. It never will. As long as it*
> *remains, there will always be a housing 'crisis'."*[44]

In my belief, as long as there exists a housing
crisis, so too there will be an inner city crisis.
The housing problem can be solved: not through a
reduction in population, but by increased investment
and reorganisation within the market. Only the political
will is lacking. Whether in turn a new crisis will then

emerge is a different question. As I have suggested
repeatedly, the city is only an adjunct of society,
and the city's problems are society's problems. Even
if the population at risk moves, we have no guarantees
that the economic climate of the next two decades will
not become more difficult for the poorly-skilled. In
that case, it is possible that the concentrations of
poverty already observed in some suburban local authority
developments and overspill estates will be exacerbated.
Should this happen, the underlying cause of the inner
area problems will be revealed, once and for all, as
the economic system within which we operate, not the
parts of the city in which we live.

NOTES AND REFERENCES: CHAPTER FIVE

1. Obvious examples here include the cost-benefit analyses,
    applied in a practical vein within the choosing of
    the Third London Airport, (see P. Hall, "Roskill, an
    analysis", New Society, January 1971), and discussed
    further in the recent Leitch Report on trunk-road
    assessment, (HMSO, 1977).

2. This is not strictly true: the field of Urban Dynamics,
    promoted by Forester, has attempted to reduce the workings
    of the city to a computer simulation model. Similarly,
    a series of Urban land-use models exist, which can deal
    with the relationships between employment, population
    and services. The extent to which such models could
    effectively be used within a planning strategy is
    doubtful however: see T.A. Broadbent, "Planning and
    profit in the urban economy", Methuen, 1977.

3. R.E. Pahl, "Whose city?", Penguin Books, 1975, pp. 4-5.

4. This area of interest is both nascent, and complicated
    which makes understanding very difficult. The most lucid
    analysis is that of David Harvey, "Social justice and the
    city", Arnold, 1973; and the quotes are taken from that
    work. He emphasises the existence of two flows of surplus
    value i.e. simply, the product of labour power, (or even
    more simply, wealth). *"The first circuit arises out of
    industrial activity and involves that simple conversion
    of naturally occurring materials and forces into objects
    and powers of utility to man. The second circuit
    involves the creation and extraction of surplus value*

> *out of speculation in property rights (or all sorts) and out of returns gained from the disbursement of fixed capital investments".* (p. 312) The first circuit is still predominant, but the relationships between the two circuits become increasingly complex, especially in the spatial context (e.g. within the city). *"The structuring of space grows more and more important as fixed capital investments become more and more important to the process of living".* (p. 310) The concentration upon speculative investment has not favoured the inner areas, except where, for example office developments have been built. It is exactly the demise of this type of speculation that Harvey has in mind when he suggests that *"the second circuit is far more crisis prone than the first, while contradiction between the two circuits is a constant source of tension"* (p. 313). This in turn leads to friction in spatial terms: for example *"the antagonism that exists between central city and suburb emerges as a major theme in American politics"* (p. 308). Importantly, the disinvestment from the inner city has resulted in a division between public and private investment in different parts of both American and British cities, which institutionalises this friction.
>
> It is interesting to note that Harvey suggests that *"to understand the circulation of surplus value is in fact to understand the way in which society works".*

5. P. Ambrose and B. Colenutt, "The property machine", Penguin Books, 1975, p. 15.

6. Ibid, p. 101.

7. See for example C. Cockburn, "The local state", Pluto Press, 1977: nationally, local expenditure based upon rates has fallen from 41% of total in 1954 to 30% in 1974 (p. 65).

8. S. Holland, "The regional problem", Macmillan, 1976.

9. CDP, "The costs of industrial change", CDP, 1977, p. 31.

10. D. Keeble, "Industrial location and planning in the U.K.", Methuen, 1976. This assumption is based upon the sheer numbers of jobs created within the Development Areas: the levels of skill involved, pay, and sex of the workforce were not, however, considered.

11. CDP, "The costs of industrial change", CDP, 1977, p. 52.

12. Ibid, p. 96.

13. Ibid, p. 94.

14. Interestingly, Ray Pahl has come to grips with this problem, and he considers that spatial, resource-type questions are likely to emerge in any political system, simply because some facilities like schools have to be put in particular places, and cannot be given to consumers directly: see "Whose city", Penguin Books, 1975.

15. Department of the Environment, "Change or decay", HMSO, 1977, p. 214.

16. Ibid, p. 215.

17. Department of the Environment, "Inner London", HMSO, 1977, p. 209.

18. This point is made by S.S. Duncan, "Self-help: the allocation of mortgages and the formation of housing sub-markets", Area 8, 4, 1976, pp. 307-15.

19. The mortgage is seen by Boddy as a means of allying the home owner with the needs of capital, which are primarily stability and investment: M. Boddy, "The structure of mortgage finance: building societies and the British social formation", Transactions, Institute of British Geographers, 1976, NS, 1, 1, pp. 58-71.

20. "Housing policy - a consultative document", HMSO, 1977, Cmnd, 6851.

21. Department of the Environment, "Inner London", HMSO, 1977, p. 209.

22. S. Marks, "In London's housing trap", New Society, 8 September 1977, p. 488.

23. See for example J.P. Macey and C.V. Baker, "Housing Management, Estates Gazette, 1965.

24. A. Thornley, "Participation in planning", Progress in Planning, Pergamon, 1977.

25. J. Craddock, "Council tenants' participation in housing management", Association of London Housing Estates, 1975, p. 100. The study was based upon work in Lambeth, Southwark, Wandsworth and the GLC estates.

26. Department of the Environment, "Unequal city", HMSO, 1977, p. 323.

27. Ibid, p. 281.

28. This issue is well covered by P. Hall, "Urban and regional planning", Penguin Books, 1975.

29. R. Coursey, "The debate on urban policy", Retailing and Planning Associates, 1977.

30. R.E. Pahl, "Whose city?", Penguin Books, 1975, p. 298.

31. J.S. Foreman-Peck and P. Gripaios, "Inner city problems and inner city policies, Regional Studies, 1977, 11, 6, p. 407.

32. Ibid, p. 410.

33. See R. Simpson, "For richer, for poorer", New Society, 10 November 1977, pp. 299-301.

34. R. Coursey, "The debate on urban policy", Retailing and Planning Associates, 1977, pp. 83-84.

35. "Policy for the inner cities", HMSO, Cmnd 6845, 1977.

36. J.S. Foreman-Peck and P. Gripaios, "Inner city problems and inner city policies", op. cit., p. 410.

37. A.R. Townsend, "The relationship of inner city problems to regional policy", Regional Studies, 1977, 11, 3, pp. 225-51.

38. Department of the Environment, "Inner London", HMSO, 1977, p. 208.

39. CDP, "The costs of industrial change", CDP, 1977, p. 96.

40. Ibid, p. 96.

41. P. Hall, "The inner cities dilemma", New Society, 3 February 1977, p. 225.

42. M. Phillips, "A smell of trouble", New Society, 9 February 1978, p. 301.

43. P. Hall, "Planning for no growth", New Society, 30 March 1978, p. 724.

44. CDP, "Profits against houses", CDP, 1976, p. 3.